INSIDE THE PSYCHE

ABDUL BASIT QAMAR

IN MEMORY OF MY BELOVED FATHER,

KHURSHID UZ ZAMAN

Contents

Preface

Welcome, dear reader! I am excited to take you on a journey "Inside the Psyche" and explore the fascinating and complex world of the human mind. The study of the psyche has intrigued scholars, philosophers, and everyday people for centuries, and with good reason. Our thoughts, feelings, and actions are governed by the intricate workings of the mind, and understanding how the psyche functions are crucial for personal growth, healthy relationships, and overall well-being.

In this book, we will embark on a journey that spans centuries and encompasses many different fields of study. We will begin by defining the concept of the psyche and exploring the importance of understanding the psyche in everyday life. From there, we will dive into the historical perspectives of the study of the psyche, examining the work of key figures such as Freud and Jung and how their theories have shaped our understanding of the mind.

But we won't stop there. We will delve into the very structure of the psyche, exploring the conscious and unconscious mind, the ego, id, and superego, and the dynamic interaction between these components. We will also examine the different stages of psychological development, from infancy to adulthood, and how our experiences and relationships shape who we are.

The mind is not static, and neither is our understanding of it. We will explore the many psychological processes that govern our perceptions, emotions, motivations, and behaviors, such as cognitive biases and heuristics. We will also examine the fascinating relationship between personality and the psyche, and how our traits and characteristics shape our thoughts and behaviors.

But what about mental health? In "Inside the Psyche," we will examine mental health disorders and the impact they have on the psyche. We will explore the role of psychotherapy in treating these disorders and how understanding the psyche can help us maintain good mental health and well-being.

As we journey through the different facets of the psyche, we will also explore the relationship between culture and the psyche. We will examine how cultural context shapes our thoughts and behaviors, and how different cultural norms can impact our understanding of the mind.

Finally, we will take a glimpse into the future of the study of the psyche, exploring the exciting advances in the field of neuroscience, cognitive psychology, and other related areas.

I hope this book will be a thought-provoking and engaging journey into the mysteries of the mind. Through understanding the psyche, we can gain insights into our behaviors and motivations, as well as those of the people around us. Whether you are a student of psychology or just a curious reader, I invite you to join me in "Inside the Psyche" and discover the many wonders of the human mind.

Acknowledgments

First and foremost, I would like to express my deepest gratitude to my friends and family for their unwavering support and encouragement throughout the writing process of this book. Their love and support have been invaluable and have made this journey possible.

I would also like to thank Mahnoor Shahid, for guiding me with her wisdom and expertise. Her motivational words and support have been instrumental in shaping the content of this book.

I would also like to thank the team at Kindle Direct Publishing (KDP), Amazon, for their hard work and dedication in bringing this book to life. Their expertise and professionalism have been essential in bringing this project to fruition.

Finally, I would like to express my appreciation to all of my readers. Your support and encouragement have been the driving force behind this book and I hope that it will be of value to you in your journey toward success.

Once again, thank you to everyone who has supported me throughout this process. I am deeply grateful for your contributions and support.

Introduction

Overview

❖ **The Concept of the Psyche**

- ✓ *Psychoanalysis*
- ✓ *Behaviorism*
- ✓ *Cognitive Psychology*
- ✓ *Neuroscience*

❖ **Importance of Understanding the Psyche**

- ✓ *Insight into Human Behavior*
- ✓ *Effective Interventions for Mental Health Disorders*
- ✓ *Improving Overall Well-being*
- ✓ *Promoting Empathy and Compassion*
- ✓ *Applications in Education*
- ✓ *Applications in Business*
- ✓ *Impact on Social Interactions and Relationships*
- ✓ *Role in Personal Development*
- ✓ *Connection to Neuroscience*
- ✓ *Interdisciplinary Approach to Understanding the Psyche*

1.1 *The Concept of the Psyche*

The concept of the psyche has a rich history, and its meaning has evolved. In ancient Greece, the term psyche was closely associated with the idea of the soul or the life force that animates a living being. The word "psukhē" was derived from the verb "psukhein," which means "to breathe." In this context, the psyche was seen as a vital essence that could be separated from the body and continue to exist after death.

In Greek mythology, Psyche was the goddess of the soul, often depicted with butterfly wings and a human face. She was associated with the idea of the soul's journey, particularly through death and rebirth.

In the medieval period, the concept of the psyche was integrated into Christian theology, where it was associated with the idea of the immortal soul. The psyche was seen as the divine spark that resided within each human being, which could be saved or damned depending on their actions in life.

In the Renaissance, the concept of the psyche underwent a significant shift, as thinkers began to question the idea of an immortal soul. Philosophers such as Rene Descartes emphasized the importance of reason and consciousness, arguing that the mind was a separate entity from the body.

In modern psychology, the term psyche has been used to refer to the totality of the human mind, including both conscious and unconscious mental processes. This definition has been shaped by the work of influential psychologists such as Sigmund Freud, who developed the psychoanalytic theory of the psyche. According to Freud, the psyche is composed of three parts: the conscious mind, the preconscious mind, and the unconscious mind. The conscious mind is part of the psyche that we are aware of, while the preconscious and unconscious minds contain information and processes that are hidden from our awareness.

Other psychologists have expanded on Freud's work, developing theories that incorporate a wider range of mental processes and factors such as emotion, cognition, and social context. While the concept of the psyche has evolved, it remains a central concept in psychology, providing a framework for understanding the complex processes that underlie human behavior and experience.

Psychologists have used various approaches to study the psyche, including psychoanalysis, behaviorism, cognitive psychology, and neuroscience. Each approach offers a unique perspective on the nature of the psyche and the processes that underlie human behavior.

- *Psychoanalysis*

Psychoanalysis is a school of psychology that was founded by Sigmund Freud in the late 19th and early 20th centuries. This approach to psychology focuses on the unconscious processes of the psyche and their influence on behavior. According to Freud, the psyche is composed of three parts: the conscious mind, the preconscious mind, and the unconscious mind.

The conscious mind represents the thoughts and feelings that we are aware of at any given moment. These thoughts and feelings are the results of our ongoing experiences and interactions with the world around us. The preconscious mind, on the other hand, contains information that is not currently in our awareness but can be brought into consciousness with effort. For example, if you are trying to remember a phone number that you recently saw, the information is in your preconscious mind and can be accessed with effort. The unconscious mind, however, contains repressed memories, desires, and fears that are not accessible to conscious awareness.

Freud believed that many psychological problems stem from conflicts between the conscious and unconscious parts of the psyche. For example, he proposed that repressed memories and desires could manifest in the form of psychological symptoms, such as anxiety or depression. According to Freud, the unconscious mind exerts a powerful influence on behavior, even though we are not aware of it.

Psychoanalysis seeks to uncover these unconscious conflicts through a variety of techniques. One such technique is free association, in which the patient is encouraged to talk about whatever comes to mind without censoring themselves. By allowing thoughts and feelings to surface without inhibition, the patient may be able to access unconscious material that has been repressed.

Another technique used in psychoanalysis is dream analysis. According to Freud, dreams are a window into the unconscious mind and can reveal repressed desires and fears. By analyzing the symbols and content of dreams, the therapist and patient may be able to gain insight into unconscious conflicts and work to resolve them.

Critics of psychoanalysis argue that it is unscientific and lacks empirical evidence. However, psychoanalysis remains an influential approach to psychology, particularly in the field of psychotherapy, where many therapists use psychoanalytic techniques to help patients gain insight into their unconscious processes and work through psychological problems.

- *Behaviorism*

Behaviorism is a school of psychology that emerged in the early 20th century, led by figures such as John Watson and B.F. Skinner. This approach to psychology emphasizes the study of observable behavior rather than internal mental processes such as thoughts and feelings. Behaviorists believe that behavior is shaped by environmental factors and that the psyche is not a separate entity but rather an emergent property of the interactions between an individual and their environment.

According to behaviorism, behavior is learned through the process of conditioning. There are two types of conditioning: classical conditioning and operant conditioning. Classical conditioning occurs when a neutral stimulus is repeatedly paired with a stimulus that elicits a natural response, such as the salivation of a dog at the sound of a bell. Over time, the neutral stimulus comes to elicit the same response as the natural stimulus. Operant conditioning, on the other hand, occurs when behavior is shaped by the consequences that follow it. If a behavior is followed by a positive consequence, such as a reward, it is more likely to be repeated in the future. If a behavior is followed by a negative consequence, such as punishment, it is less likely to be repeated.

Behaviorists believe that behavior can be explained by environmental factors alone and that internal mental processes such as thoughts and feelings are not necessary to understand behavior. They argue that the focus should be on identifying the environmental factors that shape behavior and on developing interventions to modify those factors to change behavior. For example, a behaviorist might work with a child who is afraid of dogs to gradually expose them to dogs in a safe and controlled environment, to help them overcome their fear.

Critics of behaviorism argue that it overlooks the role of internal mental processes in shaping behavior and that it does not adequately account for the complexity and richness of human experience. However, behaviorism remains an important approach to psychology, particularly in areas such as education, where the principles of behaviorism are often applied to modify behavior in a variety of contexts.

- ***Cognitive psychology***

Cognitive psychology is a branch of psychology that emphasizes the role of mental processes in shaping behavior. This approach to psychology focuses on understanding how people think, perceive, learn, and remember. Cognitive psychologists believe that the psyche is composed of mental representations or schemas, which are used to interpret and organize sensory information. These schemas can be influenced by past experiences and expectations and can in turn shape behavior.

Perception is the process by which we interpret sensory information from the environment. Cognitive psychologists study how people perceive and interpret information and how this process can influence behavior. Attention is another important mental process studied by cognitive psychologists.

Attention refers to the ability to focus on certain stimuli while ignoring others. Cognitive psychologists study how attentional processes affect behavior and how these processes can be improved through training.

Memory is also a key area of study in cognitive psychology. Cognitive psychologists study how information is encoded, stored, and retrieved in memory. They also study how memory processes can be improved through techniques such as repetition and elaboration.

Language is another important area of study in cognitive psychology. Cognitive psychologists study how language is acquired, processed, and used to communicate. They also study how language can influence behavior and how communication can be improved through techniques such as feedback and instruction.

Cognitive psychologists believe that mental processes such as perception, attention, memory, and language are interconnected and work together to shape behavior. They also believe that these mental processes can be influenced by a variety of factors, including past experiences, expectations, and context. For example, a person's schema for a particular situation can influence how they perceive and interpret new information in that situation, which can in turn shape their behavior.

Overall, cognitive psychology has had a significant impact on our understanding of the psyche and how it shapes behavior. This approach to psychology has contributed to the development of effective interventions and treatments for a range of psychological problems, such as anxiety and depression. Cognitive techniques such as cognitive restructuring and cognitive-behavioral therapy (CBT) are effective in improving mental health and well-being.

- *Neuroscience*

Neuroscience is a field of study that seeks to understand the functioning of the nervous system, including the brain, spinal cord, and peripheral nervous system. Neuroscience has made significant contributions to our understanding of the psyche by identifying the specific regions of the brain that are involved in various mental processes, such as perception, emotion, and decision-making.

One of the primary tools used by neuroscientists is brain imaging, which allows them to visualize the activity of the brain in real time. Techniques such as functional magnetic resonance imaging (fMRI) and positron emission tomography (PET) have revealed specific brain regions that are associated with particular mental processes. For example, studies have shown that the amygdala, a small almond-shaped structure in the brain, is involved in processing emotions such as fear and anxiety.

Neuroscience research has also shown that the brain is highly plastic, meaning it can change and adapt in response to experience. This has led to the development of neuroplasticity-based therapies for mental health disorders, such as cognitive behavioral therapy (CBT), which aims to retrain the brain to think differently and improve mental health.

In addition to brain imaging, neuroscientists use other techniques to study the nervous system, such as electrophysiology and neurochemistry. These methods allow researchers to investigate the electrical and chemical processes that underlie neural activity and communication.

Overall, neuroscience has significantly contributed to our understanding of the psyche by revealing the neural basis of mental processes, showing how the brain can change and adapt in response to experience, and providing insights into the mechanisms of mental health disorders.

1.2 *Importance of Understanding the Psyche*

Understanding the psyche is crucial for individuals and society as a whole. The psyche, or the totality of the human mind, encompasses a wide range of psychological processes that shape behavior, emotions, thoughts, and perceptions. By understanding these processes, we can gain valuable insights into human behavior and mental health, and develop interventions that promote well-being and social harmony.

- ### *Insight into Human Behavior*

Understanding the psyche, or the totality of the human mind is crucial for gaining insight into human behavior. Human behavior is complex and multifaceted, often influenced by a wide range of psychological processes such as perception, cognition, emotion, and motivation. By understanding these underlying psychological processes, we can better understand why people act the way they do, which can be useful in many areas of life.

Firstly, understanding the psyche can provide valuable insight into the learning process. The human mind processes information in unique ways, and understanding these processes can help teachers create effective teaching strategies that facilitate learning. For example, understanding how individuals perceive and encode information can help teachers present information in a way that maximizes understanding and retention.

Secondly, understanding the psyche can help us understand how we form and maintain relationships. Human beings are social creatures, and social interactions are an integral part of our lives. By understanding the underlying psychological processes that contribute to relationship formation and maintenance, we can develop more fulfilling relationships with others. For example, understanding the importance of empathy and effective communication can help individuals build stronger and more meaningful relationships.

Thirdly, understanding the psyche can provide insight into consumer behavior. Consumer behavior is influenced by a wide range of psychological processes such as perception, cognition, emotion, and motivation. By understanding these processes, companies can develop better marketing strategies and products that meet the needs and desires of their customers. For example, understanding how consumers perceive and evaluate products can help companies design products that are more appealing and attractive to consumers.

- ### *Effective Interventions for Mental Health Disorders*

Understanding the psyche is crucial for developing effective interventions for mental health disorders. Mental health disorders can significantly impair an individual's ability to function and lead a fulfilling life. By understanding the underlying psychological processes that contribute to these disorders, mental health professionals can develop evidence-based treatments that target these processes and improve outcomes for patients.

Mental health disorders, such as depression, anxiety, bipolar disorder, schizophrenia, and personality disorders, are complex and can have various causes, including genetics, environmental factors, and psychological processes. Therefore, understanding the psyche can help to identify the factors contributing to a particular mental health disorder and develop an appropriate intervention plan.

One of the most commonly used interventions for mental health disorders is psychotherapy, which involves talking to a trained mental health professional to understand and manage psychological problems. Different psychotherapy approaches, such as cognitive-behavioral therapy, psychodynamic therapy, and interpersonal therapy, target different aspects of psychological processes to help individuals overcome their mental health problems.

Pharmacological interventions, such as antidepressants, antipsychotics, and anxiolytics, are also commonly used to manage mental health disorders. These drugs target specific neurochemicals in the brain that are associated with mental health disorders and help to alleviate symptoms. The development of these drugs relies heavily on a better understanding of the psyche, such as the neurochemistry of the brain and the interaction of drugs with these neurochemicals.

In addition to psychotherapy and pharmacological interventions, other treatments for mental health disorders include brain stimulation techniques such as electroconvulsive therapy (ECT), transcranial magnetic stimulation (TMS), and deep brain stimulation (DBS). These techniques use electrical or magnetic currents to stimulate specific regions of the brain and modulate the underlying neural processes that contribute to mental health disorders.

- ### *Improving Overall Well-being*

Understanding the psyche is essential for improving overall well-being. Our psychological state plays a critical role in our physical health, social interactions, and overall quality of life. Therefore, it is essential to understand the psychological factors that contribute to well-being to develop effective strategies to promote mental health and prevent mental health problems.

One of the most significant ways to improve overall well-being is to understand the factors that contribute to psychological well-being. Psychological well-being refers to a state of positive psychological functioning characterized by high levels of positive emotions, engagement, meaning, positive relationships, and accomplishment. Research has identified several factors that contribute to psychological well-being, including social support, positive thinking, and effective coping strategies.

Social support refers to the emotional, informational, and practical support provided by others, such as family, friends, and community members. Social support can help individuals cope with stress, provide a sense of belonging and connectedness, and promote feelings of self-worth and value.

Positive thinking involves adopting an optimistic outlook on life, focusing on the positive aspects of situations, and engaging in positive self-talk. Positive thinking has been associated with increased resilience, better emotional regulation, and improved mental health outcomes.

Effective coping strategies involve adaptive ways of dealing with stress and difficult situations. These strategies include mindfulness meditation, physical exercise, problem-solving, and seeking social support. Developing effective coping strategies can help individuals manage stress and reduce the risk of mental health problems.

Understanding the psychological factors that contribute to well-being can help individuals take steps to improve their mental health and overall quality of life. Practices such as mindfulness meditation, cognitive restructuring, and behavioral activation have been shown to promote psychological well-being and improve mental health outcomes.

- ***Promoting Empathy and Compassion***

Understanding the psyche, or the totality of the human mind can also promote empathy and compassion towards others. By recognizing the complexity of human behavior and experience, individuals can develop a deeper appreciation for the diversity of people and the factors that influence their behavior.

One way in which understanding the psyche promotes empathy and compassion is by increasing awareness of the psychological processes that contribute to prejudice and discrimination. Research in social psychology has shown that attitudes and behaviors toward others can be influenced by various factors, such as stereotypes, social norms, and intergroup relations. By understanding these processes, individuals can become more aware of their own biases and develop more inclusive attitudes and behaviors towards people from different backgrounds.

Furthermore, understanding the psyche can help individuals recognize the impact of their behavior on others and develop a greater sense of empathy. For example, by understanding the impact of trauma on mental health, individuals can develop greater compassion towards individuals who have experienced traumatic events. By understanding the role of social support in promoting well-being, individuals can become more supportive and understanding toward others who may be going through difficult times.

In addition, understanding the psychological processes that underlie emotions can promote empathy and compassion toward others. For example, research in affective neuroscience has shown that experiencing emotions involves a complex interplay between various brain regions and neural pathways. By understanding these processes, individuals can develop a greater understanding of the emotions experienced by others and become more empathetic toward their struggles.

- ### *Applications in Education*

Understanding the psyche is crucial in the field of education as it can provide valuable insights into how students learn, process information, and interact with their environment. By understanding the psychological processes that underlie these aspects of learning, educators can develop effective teaching strategies that facilitate learning and promote academic success.

One important aspect of understanding the psyche in education is understanding how students perceive and process information. This includes factors such as attention, memory, and reasoning abilities. For example, research has shown that students are more likely to remember information when it is presented in a way that is relevant to their lives or interests, and when it is presented in a way that is consistent with their learning style preferences.

Another important aspect of understanding the psyche in education is understanding the role of motivation in learning. Motivation refers to the drive or desire to learn and can be influenced by factors such as interest in the subject matter, the perceived value of the learning experience, and self-efficacy (belief in one's ability to succeed). Understanding how motivation affects learning can help educators create learning experiences that are engaging and relevant to student's interests, and that promote a sense of competence and mastery.

Understanding the psyche in education also involves understanding the social and emotional aspects of learning. Students' social and emotional well-being can have a significant impact on their academic success and can be influenced by factors such as peer relationships, family support, and stress levels. Educators who understand these factors can create supportive learning environments that promote social and emotional well-being and facilitate learning and academic success.

• *Applications in Business*

Understanding the psyche has important applications in the field of business, particularly in marketing and consumer behavior. By understanding the psychological processes that underlie consumer behavior, businesses can develop more effective marketing strategies and products that meet the needs and desires of their target audience.

One way in which understanding the psyche can be applied in business is through the use of market research. Market research involves gathering and analyzing data on consumer behavior, attitudes, and preferences to inform business decisions. By understanding the psychological processes that influence consumer behavior, such as motivation, perception, and decision-making, businesses can develop more effective market research strategies that yield valuable insights into consumer behavior.

Another way in which understanding the psyche can be applied in business is through the development of marketing strategies that are tailored to the psychological needs and desires of consumers. For example, businesses can use psychological principles such as social proof, scarcity, and reciprocity to influence consumer behavior and increase sales. The social proof involves using testimonials or endorsements from satisfied customers to persuade potential customers to buy a product. Scarcity involves creating a sense of urgency by limiting the availability of a product. Reciprocity involves offering something of value to the customer, such as a gift, in exchange for a purchase.

Understanding the psyche can also be applied to the development of products that meet the psychological needs and desires of consumers. For example, businesses can use psychological principles such as color psychology and sensory marketing to create products that are visually appealing and emotionally engaging. Color psychology involves using colors to evoke certain emotions or associations in consumers. Sensory marketing involves engaging consumers' senses, such as sight, smell, and touch, to create a more immersive and memorable experience.

- ***Impact on Social Interactions and Relationships***

Understanding the psyche, or the totality of the human mind can have a significant impact on social interactions and relationships. By recognizing the complex interplay between various psychological processes, individuals can develop a deeper appreciation for the diversity and complexity of human experience, which can lead to greater empathy and understanding toward others.

One way in which understanding the psyche can impact social interactions and relationships is by reducing prejudice and discrimination. Prejudice and discrimination are often the results of negative attitudes towards individuals or groups based on factors such as race, gender, or sexual orientation. By understanding the psychological processes that contribute to these negative attitudes, individuals can work to develop more inclusive attitudes and behaviors towards people from different backgrounds.

Another way in which understanding the psyche can impact social interactions and relationships is by improving communication and conflict-resolution skills. Communication is a fundamental aspect of social interaction, and understanding how communication works can help individuals express themselves more effectively and avoid misunderstandings. Additionally, conflict is a common occurrence in relationships, and understanding the psychological processes that contribute to conflict can help individuals resolve disputes more effectively.

- ### *Role in Personal Development*

Understanding the psyche can play a crucial role in personal development. The psyche is a complex and multifaceted entity that encompasses various aspects of our mental and emotional lives, including our thoughts, feelings, behaviors, and motivations. By gaining a deeper understanding of these aspects, individuals can become more self-aware, which can lead to personal growth and development.

One way in which understanding the psyche can aid personal development is by identifying and addressing negative thought patterns and beliefs. Many individuals have unconscious beliefs and assumptions that can limit their potential and prevent them from achieving their goals. For example, someone may believe that they are not smart enough to pursue a certain career, or that they are not deserving of love and happiness. These beliefs can become self-fulfilling prophecies and prevent individuals from reaching their full potential.

By understanding the underlying psychological processes that contribute to these negative beliefs, individuals can challenge and replace them with more positive and empowering ones. For example, cognitive restructuring techniques can help individuals identify and challenge negative thoughts and beliefs, and replace them with more positive and realistic ones.

Another way in which understanding the psyche can aid personal development is by improving emotional regulation and resilience. Emotions play a critical role in our mental and physical health, and our ability to cope with stress and adversity. By understanding the underlying psychological processes that contribute to emotional regulation and resilience, individuals can develop effective coping strategies and improve their overall well-being.

For example, mindfulness meditation has been shown to reduce stress and improve emotional regulation by helping individuals become more aware of their thoughts and emotions, and develop a more accepting and non-judgmental attitude toward them. Similarly, developing healthy coping strategies such as exercise, social support, and relaxation techniques can help individuals manage stress and build resilience.

Finally, understanding the psyche can aid personal development by promoting self-compassion and acceptance. Many individuals struggle with self-criticism and self-judgment, which can prevent them from fully accepting and loving themselves. By understanding the underlying psychological processes that contribute to self-criticism and self-judgment, individuals can develop a more compassionate and accepting attitude toward themselves.

For example, self-compassion exercises such as writing self-compassionate letters or practicing loving-kindness meditation can help individuals develop a more positive and accepting attitude towards themselves. This can lead to greater self-esteem, self-confidence, and overall well-being.

- ### *Connection to Neuroscience*

The field of neuroscience is closely related to the study of the psyche, as it seeks to understand how the brain and nervous system contribute to behavior, thoughts, and emotions. Advances in neuroscience have helped researchers to gain a better understanding of the biological basis of various psychological processes and disorders, including perception, attention, memory, emotion, and motivation.

For example, neuroimaging techniques such as functional magnetic resonance imaging (fMRI) and electroencephalography (EEG) have allowed researchers to study brain activity in real time while individuals engage in various tasks or experience emotions. These techniques have been used to identify neural circuits and networks that underlie various psychological processes, such as the amygdala's role in processing emotional information and the prefrontal cortex's role in decision-making and cognitive control.

Furthermore, neuroscience research has led to the development of new treatments for mental health disorders. For example, selective serotonin reuptake inhibitors (SSRIs), which are commonly used to treat depression and anxiety disorders, work by increasing the availability of serotonin in the brain. This neurotransmitter is known to play a role in regulating mood and emotion.

In summary, understanding the connection between the psyche and neuroscience is crucial for gaining a more comprehensive understanding of human behavior and developing effective treatments for mental health disorders.

- ***Interdisciplinary Approach to Understanding the Psyche***

The interdisciplinary approach to understanding the psyche involves integrating knowledge and perspectives from different fields, including psychology, neuroscience, philosophy, sociology, anthropology, and biology, to gain a more comprehensive understanding of the human mind and behavior.

Each discipline offers a unique perspective on the psyche and how it functions, and by integrating these perspectives, we can gain a more holistic understanding of the complexity of the human experience. For example, psychology provides insights into mental processes and behavior, while neuroscience helps us understand the biological underpinnings of these processes.

Philosophy can contribute to our understanding of the nature of consciousness and the self, while sociology and anthropology can provide insights into how culture and social structures influence behavior and psychological processes.

Biology can help us understand the genetic and physiological factors that contribute to mental health disorders and other aspects of the psyche.

By combining these different perspectives, we can gain a more nuanced understanding of the psyche, it's functioning, and its impact on behavior, mental health, and social interactions. This interdisciplinary approach can lead to the development of more effective interventions for mental health disorders, as well as more comprehensive educational and business strategies that take into account the complexity of human behavior and motivation.

In conclusion, understanding the psyche is essential for gaining insights into human behavior, developing effective interventions for mental health disorders, improving overall well-being, and promoting empathy and compassion towards others. The various psychological processes that comprise the psyche are interrelated and complex, and understanding them can lead to a deeper understanding of the human experience and facilitate social harmony and well-being.

Historical Perspectives

Overview

❖ **Historical background**

❖ ***Key figures in the Study of the Psyche***

✓ *Sigmund Freud*
✓ *Carl Jung*
✓ *B.F. Skinner*
✓ *William James*
✓ *Abraham Maslow*
✓ *Ivan Pavlov*
✓ *Jean Piaget*
✓ *Erik Erikson*
✓ *Lev Vygotsky*
✓ *Karen Horney*
✓ *John B. Watson*
✓ *Hermann Ebbinghaus*
✓ *Noam Chomsky*
✓ *Mary Ainsworth*
✓ *Albert Bandura*

2.1 Historical background

The study of the psyche, or the human mind and its functions, has a long and complex history that spans millennia. From the earliest civilizations to modern times, thinkers and scholars have attempted to understand the workings of the mind and how it shapes human behavior.

The earliest recorded attempts to study the psyche date back to ancient civilizations such as Greece, Egypt, and China. In Greece, philosophers such as Plato and Aristotle explored questions related to the nature of the mind and its relationship to the body. Plato believed that the mind was immortal and existed independently of the physical body, while Aristotle believed that the mind was an aspect of the body and could not exist without it.

In Egypt, the study of the psyche was closely linked to religion and spirituality. The Egyptians believed in the concept of ka, or the immortal soul, which was thought to be responsible for a person's personality and behavior. Similarly, in China, the study of the psyche was closely tied to Taoism and Confucianism, which emphasized the importance of cultivating a harmonious relationship between the mind, body, and spirit.

During the middle Ages, the study of the psyche was largely influenced by the teachings of the Christian church. Theologians such as St. Augustine and St. Thomas Aquinas explored questions related to the nature of the soul and its relationship to God. They believed that the mind was an aspect of the soul and that the soul was responsible for guiding a person's behavior.

The Renaissance marked a significant shift in the study of the psyche. Renaissance thinkers such as Leonardo da Vinci and Michelangelo emphasized the importance of observation and empirical research in understanding the mind. They believed that the mind was a complex machine that could be studied and understood through careful observation and experimentation.

The Enlightenment brought about even more significant changes in the study of the psyche. Philosophers such as John Locke and David Hume emphasized the importance of reason and empirical evidence in understanding the mind. They believed that the mind was a blank slate at birth and that all knowledge was acquired through experience.

The 19th and 20th centuries saw the emergence of psychology as a distinct scientific discipline. The founding fathers of psychology, such as Wilhelm Wundt and Sigmund Freud, sought to understand the mind through scientific methods such as observation, experimentation, and psychoanalysis. They believed that the mind was a complex structure that could be studied and understood through careful observation and analysis of behavior and mental processes.

In the 21st century, the study of the psyche continues to evolve and expand. Advances in neuroscience, cognitive science, and artificial intelligence have led to new insights into the workings of the mind and its relationship to behavior. Today, researchers and scholars continue to explore questions related to the nature of consciousness, the relationship between the mind and the brain, and the potential for artificial intelligence to replicate human thought processes.

In a nutshell, the study of the psyche has a rich and complex history that spans millennia. From ancient civilizations to modern times, thinkers and scholars have attempted to understand the workings of the mind and how it shapes human behavior. While our understanding of the psyche has evolved and expanded over time, the quest to understand the nature of the mind remains as relevant and important today as it was thousands of years ago.

2.2 Key figures in the Study of the Psyche

The study of the psyche, or the human mind and its functions, has been shaped and influenced by many key figures throughout history. These individuals have contributed to the development of psychological theory and practice and have had a significant impact on our understanding of the mind and its relationship to behavior. Let's explore some of the key figures in the development of the study of the psyche, including Sigmund Freud, Carl Jung, and B.F. Skinner, and more.

- ### Sigmund Freud

Sigmund Freud is widely regarded as one of the most influential figures in the development of modern psychology. Born in Austria in 1856, Freud developed a revolutionary theory of the mind that emphasized the importance of the unconscious in shaping human behavior. He believed that many of our thoughts, feelings, and behaviors were driven by unconscious desires and conflicts that were rooted in childhood experiences and that these repressed desires could manifest in a variety of ways, including dreams, fantasies, and neurotic symptoms.

One of the key components of Freud's theory was his belief in the existence of three levels of consciousness: the conscious, preconscious, and unconscious. The conscious level consists of thoughts and perceptions that are currently in our awareness, while the preconscious contains information that can be easily brought to consciousness, such as memories or stored knowledge. The unconscious, on the other hand, contains repressed or unacceptable desires and memories that are typically outside of conscious awareness but can still influence behavior.

To explore the unconscious, Freud developed a range of techniques, including free association, dream analysis, and transference. Free association involved encouraging patients to speak freely about whatever came to mind, without censoring or editing their thoughts. Dream analysis involved exploring the hidden meanings and symbols in a patient's dreams, which Freud believed could provide insight into unconscious desires and conflicts. Transference involved patients projecting their feelings and emotions onto their therapist, which could provide valuable information about their unconscious processes.

Freud's work had a profound impact on the field of psychology, inspiring the development of psychoanalysis as a therapeutic approach. Psychoanalysis involves exploring unconscious processes and unresolved conflicts as a means of addressing mental illness and emotional distress. Freud's theories also inspired the development of other schools of thought, including neo-Freudian and psychodynamic theories.

However, Freud's theories have also been the subject of much criticism and controversy. One of the most significant critiques of Freud's work concerns his views on sexuality.

Freud believed that sexual desires and conflicts were at the root of many psychological problems, and that repressed sexuality could lead to neurotic symptoms and mental illness. This view was considered scandalous and provocative at the time and remains a controversial aspect of Freud's work to this day.

Another critique of Freud's work concerns his methods of treatment, which included the use of free association and dream analysis to explore unconscious processes. Some critics argue that these methods lack scientific rigor and are too subjective to be considered valid forms of therapy. Others have criticized Freud's emphasis on the therapist-patient relationship, which some argue can create a power imbalance that may be exploitative or unethical.

Despite these critiques, Freud's work remains a significant and influential part of the history of psychology. His theories and methods have inspired countless researchers and clinicians, and continue to shape our understanding of the mind and its relationship to behavior. Whether one agrees or disagrees with Freud's ideas, there can be no denying the impact that his work has had on the field of psychology and our understanding of the human psyche.

- ***Carl Jung***

Carl Jung was a Swiss psychiatrist and psychoanalyst who made significant contributions to the study of the psyche. Born in 1875, Jung developed a theory of the psyche that emphasized the importance of the collective unconscious in shaping human behavior. He believed that the collective unconscious was a repository of universal symbols, archetypes, and instincts that were shared by all humans and that could be accessed through dreams, myths, and other forms of cultural expression.

Jung's theory of the psyche was heavily influenced by his own experiences as a psychotherapist and his interest in spirituality and the occult. He believed that the unconscious was not simply a repository of repressed desires and memories, as Freud believed, but was also a source of creativity, intuition, and spirituality. According to Jung, the unconscious contained both personal and collective elements, and the collective unconscious was responsible for the universal themes and motifs that appear in myths, fairy tales, and other forms of cultural expression.

Jung developed a range of techniques for exploring the unconscious, including dream analysis, active imagination, and the use of archetypes. Dream analysis involved exploring the symbols and images that appeared in a patient's dreams, which Jung believed could provide insight into the unconscious processes that were influencing their behavior. Active imagination involved engaging in a form of controlled daydreaming, where patients could interact with their unconscious and explore its contents. Archetypes were universal symbols and patterns of behavior that were shared by all humans and were thought to be inherited from our ancestors.

Jung's work had a significant impact on the development of analytical psychology, a therapeutic approach that emphasizes the exploration of unconscious processes and the integration of conscious and unconscious aspects of the psyche. Analytical psychology differs from Freudian psychoanalysis in that it places less emphasis on sexuality and early childhood experiences and more emphasis on the role of spirituality, creativity, and personal growth in psychological development.

However, like Freud, Jung's theories have also been the subject of criticism and controversy. Some critics have argued that his theories lack scientific rigor and are too subjective to be considered valid forms of therapy. Others have criticized his views on spirituality and the occult, which they view as unscientific and potentially dangerous.

Despite these critiques, Jung's work remains an important and influential part of the history of psychology. His theories and techniques have inspired countless researchers and clinicians, and continue to shape our understanding of the human psyche. Whether one agrees or disagrees with Jung's ideas, there can be no denying the impact that his work has had on the field of psychology and our understanding of the human experience.

- ### *B.F. Skinner*

B.F. Skinner was an American psychologist who is widely recognized as one of the most influential figures in the development of behaviorism. Skinner's work focused on the study of observable, measurable responses to environmental stimuli, and he believed that behavior could be understood through the principles of operant conditioning.

Skinner argued that behavior was shaped by its consequences, with positive consequences reinforcing behaviors and negative consequences punishing them. One of Skinner's most famous experimental techniques was the Skinner box, a device used to study the relationship between behavior and its consequences. The Skinner box was designed to study animal behavior, and it allowed researchers to control environmental stimuli and measure the animal's responses. By manipulating the consequences of behavior, Skinner was able to demonstrate the principles of operant conditioning and how they could be used to shape behavior.

Skinner's work had a significant impact on the development of behavior therapy, a therapeutic approach that emphasizes the use of reinforcement and other behavioral techniques to modify problematic behaviors. Behavior therapy is effective in treating a wide range of disorders, including anxiety, depression, and substance abuse.

However, Skinner's theories have also been the subject of criticism and controversy, particularly about his views on free will and the role of the individual in shaping their behavior. Critics argue that Skinner's emphasis on environmental factors ignores the role of individual agency and choice in shaping behavior. They also question the ethics of using behavioral techniques to modify behavior, arguing that it can be manipulative and coercive.

Despite these criticisms, Skinner's work remains an important and influential part of the history of psychology. His theories and techniques have had a significant impact on the field of behaviorism and the development of behavior therapy. Skinner's emphasis on the importance of empirical research and measurable outcomes has also had a lasting impact on the field of psychology as a whole, and his legacy continues to influence the study of the psyche today.

- ### *William James*

William James (1842-1910) was an American philosopher and psychologist who is widely regarded as one of the most important figures in the development of modern psychology. He is often referred to as the father of American psychology and was a major influence on the development of functionalism, a school of psychology that focused on how the mind adapts to its environment.

James was born in New York City in 1842 and grew up in a family of intellectuals. He studied philosophy and medicine at Harvard University, where he became interested in the workings of the mind. He went on to become a professor of psychology and philosophy at Harvard and wrote several influential books on psychology, including "The Principles of Psychology" (1890).

James's theory of the mind emphasized the importance of consciousness in shaping human behavior. He argued that the mind was not simply a passive receptacle of sensory information, but an active agent that constantly interacted with its environment. He believed that consciousness was constantly evolving and changing and that it was shaped by our experiences, emotions, and beliefs.

One of James's most important contributions to psychology was his development of functionalism, which focused on how the mind adapted to its environment. He argued that the purpose of the mind was to help us adapt to our surroundings and that our behavior was shaped by our environment and our past experiences. He also believed that the mind could change and adapt to new situations, which he referred to as plasticity. James was also interested in the study of emotions and argued that they played an important role in shaping human behavior. He believed that emotions were not simply a response to external stimuli, but were an integral part of the mind and played an active role in shaping our thoughts and behaviors.

James's influence on psychology can still be felt today, particularly in the field of cognitive psychology. His emphasis on the importance of consciousness and the adaptive nature of the mind has been influential in shaping our understanding of how the mind works. He was also a strong advocate of interdisciplinary research and believed that psychology should be studied in conjunction with other disciplines, such as philosophy and biology.

Overall, William James's contributions to the study of the psyche were significant and enduring. His emphasis on the importance of consciousness and the adaptive nature of the mind has helped shape our understanding of the mind and its relationship to behavior. His legacy continues to influence modern psychology and his ideas remain a vital part of the discipline.

- ### *Abraham Maslow*

Abraham Maslow was an American psychologist who was born in 1908 and is best known for his development of the hierarchy of needs theory. Maslow was a humanistic psychologist who believed in the inherent goodness of people and that individuals have a natural tendency to strive toward personal growth and self-actualization.

Maslow's hierarchy of needs is a theory that suggests that people have a series of needs that must be met for them to achieve a state of self-actualization. The hierarchy is often represented as a pyramid, with the most basic physiological needs at the bottom and self-actualization at the top. The lower levels of the pyramid include physiological needs, safety needs, and love and belonging needs, while the higher levels include esteem needs and self-actualization.

Maslow argued that individuals must have their basic physiological and safety needs met before they can move on to higher-level needs. He believed that once people had their basic needs met, they could begin to focus on developing their self-esteem and achieving personal growth. Ultimately, Maslow believed that the goal of human life was to achieve self-actualization, which he defined as the realization of one's full potential and the achievement of personal fulfillment.

Maslow's work had a significant impact on the field of psychology, particularly in the development of humanistic psychology. This approach to psychology emphasizes the importance of the individual, their personal experiences, and their capacity for self-determination and personal growth. Humanistic psychology has been used in a variety of therapeutic settings, including counseling, education, and organizational development.

Despite its popularity, Maslow's hierarchy of needs has also been the subject of criticism and controversy. Some researchers have argued that the theory is too simplistic and that it fails to take into account the complex nature of human motivation. Others have criticized the hierarchy for being culturally biased, as it is based on Maslow's observations of people living in the United States and may not apply to people in other cultures. Regardless of its limitations, Maslow's work remains an important contribution to the field of psychology and continues to influence research and practice today. His emphasis on the importance of personal growth, self-actualization, and the inherent goodness of people has inspired countless individuals to strive toward their full potential and achieve a more meaningful and fulfilling life.

- ### *Ivan Pavlov*

Ivan Pavlov (1849-1936) was a Russian physiologist and psychologist who is best known for his pioneering work in the field of classical conditioning. Pavlov was born in the city of Ryazan in Russia and studied medicine at the University of Saint Petersburg. After completing his degree, he began studying the digestive system of dogs at the Institute of Experimental Medicine in Saint Petersburg.

Pavlov's initial interest was in studying the digestive system, but he soon became interested in how animals learn and respond to stimuli. In 1903, Pavlov began conducting experiments with dogs to investigate the process of classical conditioning.

His work focused on understanding how a neutral stimulus, such as the sound of a bell, could become associated with a reflex response, such as salivating in response to food.

Pavlov's experiments involved placing a dog in a harness and collecting its saliva in a measuring tube. He would then present the dog with food, which caused the dog to salivate. Over time, Pavlov noticed that the dog began to salivate in response to other stimuli that were previously neutral, such as the sound of a bell that was rung before the presentation of food.

Through this repeated pairing of the neutral stimulus (the sound of the bell) with the presentation of food, Pavlov was able to condition the dog to salivate in response to the bell alone, without the presence of food. This process of classical conditioning became a fundamental concept in psychology and has been used to explain a wide range of human behaviors, from phobias to addiction.

Pavlov's work had a significant impact on the field of psychology and inspired the development of behaviorism, a school of psychology that emphasizes the role of environmental factors in shaping behavior. His work also had practical applications, such as in the development of behavioral therapies for phobias and other anxiety disorders.

In addition to his work on classical conditioning, Pavlov also made important contributions to the study of the nervous system and digestive processes. He received numerous awards and honors for his contributions to science and remains a significant figure in the history of psychology and physiology.

- ### *Jean Piaget*

Jean Piaget was a Swiss psychologist who made significant contributions to the study of cognitive development. Born in 1896, he began his career as a biologist before turning to psychology. Piaget is best known for his theory of cognitive development, which has had a profound influence on the field of psychology and education.

Piaget's theory of cognitive development posits that children go through four distinct stages of cognitive development, each characterized by specific ways of thinking and understanding the world. The four stages are the sensorimotor stage (birth to 2 years old), the preoperational stage (2 to 7 years old), the concrete operational stage (7 to 11 years old), and the formal operational stage (11 years old and beyond).

In the sensorimotor stage, children learn through their senses and movements, gradually developing an understanding of object permanence (the realization that objects continue to exist even when they cannot be seen). In the preoperational stage, children begin to use symbols to represent objects and develop language skills but still struggle with concepts such as conservation (the understanding that quantity does not change even if the appearance changes).

In the concrete operational stage, children begin to think logically and understand concepts such as conservation and cause-and-effect relationships. Finally, in the formal operational stage, children can think abstractly and engage in hypothetical reasoning.

Piaget's theory has had a significant impact on both psychology and education. His emphasis on the importance of cognitive development in childhood has led to changes in the way children are taught and educated. Piaget also emphasized the importance of active learning and discovery in the learning process, which has influenced educational practices such as project-based learning and experiential learning.

While Piaget's theory has been influential, it has also been the subject of criticism and debate. Some researchers have argued that Piaget underestimated children's cognitive abilities, while others have questioned the universality of his stages of development. Despite these criticisms, Piaget's work remains an important contribution to our understanding of cognitive development and its implications for education and child development.

• *Erik Erikson Jean Piaget*

Erik Erikson was a prominent psychoanalyst who developed a theory of psychosocial development that emphasized the importance of social and cultural factors in shaping human behavior.

Born in Germany in 1902, Erikson immigrated to the United States in the 1930s and became a U.S. citizen in 1940. He studied psychoanalysis with Anna Freud, the daughter of Sigmund Freud, and later worked at several universities and clinics in the United States.

Erikson's theory of psychosocial development expanded on Freud's theory of psychosexual development, which emphasized the importance of biological factors in shaping human behavior. Erikson argued that social and cultural factors, such as family dynamics, cultural values, and historical context, also played a crucial role in shaping human development.

Erikson's theory of psychosocial development has had a significant impact on the field of psychology and has been applied in a range of settings, including clinical practice, education, and organizational development. His emphasis on the importance of social and cultural factors in shaping human behavior has helped to broaden our understanding of human development and the complex interplay between biology, culture, and social experience.

- *Lev Vygotsky*

Lev Vygotsky (1896-1934) was a Soviet psychologist and social constructivist who developed a theory of sociocultural development. He was born in present-day Belarus and grew up during a time of political and social upheaval in Russia. Vygotsky was interested in understanding how cultural and social factors shape human cognition and behavior, and his work had a significant impact on the fields of developmental psychology, education, and linguistics.

Vygotsky believed that cognitive development is shaped by social and cultural factors and that learning occurs through social interaction and collaboration. He argued that children are active participants in their learning and that they construct knowledge through interactions with their social and cultural environment. According to Vygotsky, the culture and language of a society provide the tools for learning and problem-solving, and these tools are transmitted from one generation to the next through social interaction.

Vygotsky developed the concept of the zone of proximal development (ZPD), which refers to the difference between what a child can do on their own and what they can do with the help of a more knowledgeable other. He believed that learning occurs when a child can engage in activities within their ZPD, with the guidance and support of a teacher or more skilled peer. Vygotsky also emphasized the importance of play in cognitive development, arguing that play provides a context for learning and problem-solving.

Vygotsky's work had a significant impact on the fields of education and child development. His ideas about the role of social and cultural factors in cognitive development have been influential in shaping educational practices and curricula. Vygotsky's emphasis on the importance of social interaction and collaboration in learning has also had a lasting impact on the field of educational psychology.

However, Vygotsky's work was largely unknown outside of the Soviet Union during his lifetime, and it was not until many years after his death that his ideas began to gain wider recognition in the West. Today, Vygotsky's theory of sociocultural development is recognized as one of the major contributions to the field of developmental psychology, and his ideas continue to be influential in shaping research and practice in education and child development.

- ### *Karen Horney*

Karen Horney was a pioneering psychoanalyst who made significant contributions to the field of psychology, particularly in the area of neurosis. Born in Germany in 1885, Horney trained as a psychiatrist and became interested in psychoanalysis after meeting Sigmund Freud in 1910. However, she eventually became critical of some of Freud's theories, particularly his emphasis on the role of unconscious conflicts in shaping behavior.

Horney believed that neurosis was caused by interpersonal conflicts and the failure to meet basic needs for love and security, rather than by unconscious conflicts as Freud had argued. She argued that people who experienced a lack of love and security in childhood were more likely to develop neurotic behaviors as adults. Horney also believed that gender roles and cultural expectations played a significant role in the development of neurosis.

Horney's theory of neurosis emphasized the importance of self-awareness and personal growth in overcoming neurotic behaviors. She believed that people needed to develop a sense of inner security and a capacity for self-regulation to achieve psychological health. Horney also emphasized the importance of social support and healthy relationships in promoting mental health.

Horney's work had a significant impact on the field of psychology and inspired the development of humanistic and existential approaches to therapy. However, her theories have also been the subject of criticism and controversy, particularly about her views on gender and the role of social and cultural factors in shaping behavior. Despite these criticisms, Horney's ideas continue to influence the study and treatment of neurosis and other psychological disorders.

- ### *John B. Watson*

John B. Watson was an American psychologist who is widely regarded as one of the founders of behaviorism. He was born in 1878 in Greenville, South Carolina, and began his career in psychology in the early 1900s. Watson's work had a significant impact on the field of psychology, particularly in the area of learning theory.

Watson believed that behavior could be understood through the study of observable responses to environmental stimuli. He rejected the idea that behavior was influenced by unconscious processes or innate drives, which had been central to the psychoanalytic theories of Sigmund Freud and others. Instead, Watson argued that behavior was learned through a process of conditioning, in which specific environmental stimuli were associated with particular responses.

One of Watson's most famous experiments was the Little Albert experiment, which he conducted with his graduate student, Rosalie Rayner, in 1920.

In the experiment, Watson and Rayner conditioned an infant known as Little Albert to fear a white rat by pairing the presentation of the rat with a loud noise. After repeated pairings, Little Albert began to show signs of fear in response to the rat alone, as well as to other white, furry objects.

Watson's work on behaviorism had a significant impact on the field of psychology, particularly in the area of learning theory. He developed several key principles of learning, including classical conditioning, which involves the association of two stimuli, and operant conditioning, which involves the association of behavior with its consequences.

However, Watson's theories have also been the subject of criticism and controversy. Some critics have argued that his emphasis on observable behavior failed to take into account the complexity of human experience, particularly the role of cognitive processes in shaping behavior. Others have criticized his experimental methods, particularly his use of animals and human subjects without their informed consent.

Despite these criticisms, Watson's work on behaviorism had a lasting impact on the field of psychology, particularly in the areas of learning theory and behavior therapy. His emphasis on the study of observable behavior remains influential today and continues to inform the development of new approaches to understanding and treating psychological disorders.

• *Hermann Ebbinghaus*

Hermann Ebbinghaus was a German psychologist who is widely recognized as one of the pioneers of the field of memory research. Born in 1850 in Germany, Ebbinghaus spent much of his early academic career studying philosophy and languages. It was not until he was in his mid-twenties that he became interested in psychology and began conducting experiments on memory.

Ebbinghaus is best known for his groundbreaking work on memory, which he conducted over several years in the late 1800s. His experiments focused on the capacity of memory and the process of forgetting. He developed several innovative techniques for measuring memory capacity and retention, including the use of nonsense syllables.

One of Ebbinghaus's most important contributions to the field of memory research was the development of the forgetting curve. The forgetting curve is a graphical representation of the rate at which information is forgotten over time.

Ebbinghaus discovered that the forgetting curve was a steep decline in memory retention in the first few hours after learning new information, followed by a more gradual decline over time.

Ebbinghaus's work on memory and the forgetting curve laid the groundwork for the development of cognitive psychology as a field of study. His experiments provided the first empirical evidence that human memory is not perfect and that forgetting is an important aspect of the memory process. He also demonstrated that memory capacity and retention could be measured and quantified, paving the way for future research in this area.

Ebbinghaus's work on memory has had a lasting impact on psychology and cognitive science. His theories and techniques continue to be studied and refined by researchers today, and his contributions have helped to shape our understanding of the complex process of human memory.

- ### *Noam Chomsky*

Noam Chomsky is one of the most influential linguists and cognitive psychologists of the 20th century. He is widely known for his theories on language acquisition and his criticisms of behaviorism, which dominated psychology in the mid-20th century.

Chomsky's theory of language acquisition, known as generative grammar, proposed that humans have an innate ability to understand and produce language. He argued that language is not simply a set of learned responses to environmental stimuli, but rather an innate capacity that is guided by a set of rules and principles that are hard-wired into the brain. According to Chomsky, all human languages share a universal grammar or a set of underlying rules and principles that are common to all languages.

Chomsky's ideas on language acquisition challenged the prevailing behaviorist view, which held that language development was a result of reinforcement and conditioning. Chomsky argued that the complexity and creativity of human language could not be explained by behaviorist principles, and instead proposed that language development was guided by an innate set of rules and principles that allowed humans to create an infinite number of sentences.

Chomsky's work on language acquisition has had a profound impact on the fields of linguistics, psychology, and cognitive science. His theories have led to a rethinking of the relationship between language and the mind, and have opened up new avenues of research into the nature of human cognition and the brain.

In addition to his work on language acquisition, Chomsky has been a vocal critic of US foreign policy and a prominent political activist. He has written extensively on topics such as media propaganda, human rights, and the Israeli-Palestinian conflict. Despite the controversy surrounding some of his political views, Chomsky's contributions to the fields of linguistics and cognitive psychology have been widely recognized and celebrated.

- ## *Mary Ainsworth*

Mary Ainsworth was a developmental psychologist who is best known for her work on attachment theory. She was born in 1913 in Glendale, Ohio, and received her Ph.D. in psychology from the University of Toronto in 1939.

Ainsworth is most famous for developing the Strange Situation, a laboratory procedure used to study attachment in infants. The procedure involves a series of separations and reunions between an infant and their caregiver and is designed to measure the quality of attachment between them. Through her research using the Strange Situation, Ainsworth identified three main attachment styles: secure attachment, anxious-ambivalent attachment, and avoidant attachment.

Ainsworth's work on attachment theory was heavily influenced by the earlier research of John Bowlby, who argued that the quality of early attachments between infants and their caregivers can have long-lasting effects on emotional and social development. Ainsworth's research expanded on Bowlby's work by providing a detailed framework for understanding the different types of attachment relationships that can form between infants and caregivers.

Ainsworth's research showed that infants who have a secure attachment to their caregiver tend to be more confident, independent, and socially competent in later life. Infants with anxious-ambivalent attachment tend to be more anxious and dependent, while those with avoidant attachment tend to be more withdrawn and emotionally detached. Later research has also identified a fourth attachment style, disorganized attachment, which is characterized by conflicting behaviors and responses to the caregiver.

In addition to her work on attachment theory, Ainsworth made other significant contributions to the field of developmental psychology. She was a pioneer in the study of maternal sensitivity, which refers to a mother's ability to perceive and respond appropriately to her infant's emotional needs. She also researched the effects of maternal depression and stress on infant development.

Ainsworth's work has had a profound impact on our understanding of the importance of early attachment relationships in shaping emotional and social development. Her research has been used to inform interventions and programs designed to support healthy attachment relationships between infants and their caregivers.

- ***Albert Bandura***

Albert Bandura is a Canadian-American psychologist born in 1925, who is widely known for his contributions to the field of social learning theory. Bandura's theory emphasized the role of cognitive processes in learning and highlighted the importance of observation, imitation, and modeling in shaping behavior.

Bandura's theory of social learning challenged traditional behaviorist theories that suggested that all behavior is shaped solely by the environment. Instead, he argued that people learn through a combination of environmental factors and cognitive processes, including attention, memory, and motivation. In his view, individuals are active agents who can choose to behave in certain ways based on their understanding of the consequences of their actions.

One of Bandura's most famous contributions to psychology was his Bobo doll experiment. In this study, children observed an adult model behaving aggressively toward an inflatable Bobo doll. The study found that children who observed the aggressive model were more likely to behave aggressively when allowed to play with the same doll. Bandura's findings suggested that people learn not only by experiencing the consequences of their behavior but also by observing the behavior of others and the consequences that result from it.

Bandura also developed the concept of self-efficacy, which refers to an individual's belief in their ability to perform a specific task or behavior. According to Bandura, self-efficacy is influenced by four factors: mastery experiences, social modeling, social persuasion, and physiological and affective states. Individuals with high self-efficacy are more likely to take on challenging tasks and persist in the face of difficulties.

In addition to his contributions to social learning theory, Bandura also conducted research on topics such as aggression, moral development, and the psychology of human agency. His work has had a significant impact on the field of psychology and has influenced the development of other theories, such as cognitive-behavioral therapy.

Bandura has been recognized for his contributions to psychology with numerous awards, including the American Psychological Association's Award for Distinguished Scientific Contributions, the National Medal of Science, and the Lifetime Achievement Award from the Association for Psychological Science. He continues to be an influential figure in psychology, and his work remains a topic of study and debate among scholars and practitioners in the field.

The Structure of the Psyche

Overview

❖ ***Exploring different Components of the Psyche***

- ✓ *Conscious mind*
- ✓ *Subconscious mind*
- ✓ *Unconscious mind*
- ✓ *Id*
- ✓ *Ego*
- ✓ *Super-ego*

❖ ***The Interaction between Id, Ego and Super-ego***

- ✓ *Id and Ego*
- ✓ *Id and Super-ego*
- ✓ *Ego and Super-ego*

3.1 *Exploring different Components of the Psyche*

Exploring the different components of the psyche involves a deep and comprehensive examination of these various aspects, including the conscious, subconscious, and unconscious mind, the ego, the id, and the superego. By understanding these different components, we can gain insight into our psychological makeup and better understand the motivations and behaviors of those around us. Ultimately, exploring the psyche can lead to greater self-awareness and personal growth, allowing us to live more fulfilling and meaningful lives.

- ### *Conscious mind*

The conscious mind is the aspect of our psyche that is responsible for our subjective experience of the world. It includes our thoughts, emotions, and perceptions, as well as our sense of self and agency. Consciousness is a fundamental aspect of human experience, and it has been the subject of intense study and debate within the fields of psychology, neuroscience, and philosophy.

One of the central questions regarding consciousness is how it arises from the physical processes of the brain. While the precise neural mechanisms that underlie consciousness are still not fully understood, researchers have identified various brain regions and neural networks that are thought to be involved in conscious experience. For example, the prefrontal cortex, which is located at the front of the brain, is thought to be involved in executive functioning and decision-making, while the parietal cortex, which is located near the top and back of the brain, is involved in spatial processing and perception.

In addition to these brain regions, researchers have also identified various neural networks that are thought to be involved in different aspects of conscious experience. For example, the default mode network, which includes the medial prefrontal cortex and the posterior cingulate cortex, is active when we are not engaged in any specific task and is thought to be involved in self-reflection and introspection. Other networks, such as the salience network and the attentional networks, are thought to be involved in processes such as attention and emotion.

Consciousness is also intimately related to the phenomenon of attention, which is the ability to selectively attend to certain stimuli while ignoring others. Attention is thought to be a critical aspect of consciousness because it allows us to focus on the aspects of our environment that are most relevant to our goals and interests. Attention is also thought to be closely related to consciousness because it allows us to be aware of our mental states and to direct our thoughts and actions accordingly.

The conscious mind plays a critical role in decision-making and problem-solving. It allows us to weigh the pros and cons of different options and to choose the course of action that is most aligned with our goals and values. However, the conscious mind is not always the sole determinant of our behavior. Research has shown that unconscious factors, such as past experiences and implicit biases, can also influence our decisions and actions.

In conclusion, the conscious mind is a complex and multifaceted aspect of our psyche that is responsible for our subjective experience of the world. It is intimately related to various brain regions and neural networks, and it plays a central role in processes such as attention, decision-making, and problem-solving. However, it is important to recognize that the conscious mind is not always the sole determinant of our behavior and that unconscious factors can also influence our thoughts and actions.

- ### *Subconscious mind*

The subconscious mind is an important concept in psychology that refers to the part of the mind that is not fully conscious but still influences our thoughts, feelings, and behaviors. It is often used interchangeably with the term "unconscious mind," although some theorists make a distinction between the two.

The subconscious mind is believed to be the repository of information that is not immediately available to conscious awareness. This can include memories that we may have forgotten or repressed, as well as emotions, desires, and motivations that are not fully conscious but still influence our behavior. This is because our brains process a vast amount of information at any given moment, much of which is not consciously attended to. This information is still processed by the brain and can influence our behavior without us being aware of it.

For example, imagine that you have a fear of flying that you cannot explain. You may have no conscious memory of a traumatic experience on an airplane, but your subconscious mind may still be reacting to the fear and anxiety associated with flying. Similarly, if you have a recurring dream about a particular place or person, it may be a manifestation of unconscious thoughts or emotions that are influencing your behavior.

The subconscious mind is believed to be particularly influential in shaping our habitual behaviors and automatic responses. This can include everything from the way we walk and talk to the way we react to stressful situations. Habits and routines can become ingrained in the subconscious mind over time, making them difficult to change without conscious effort.

While the subconscious mind is not fully accessible to conscious awareness, some theorists believe that it can be accessed through techniques such as hypnosis, meditation, or dream analysis. These techniques are thought to allow individuals to bypass conscious awareness and gain insight into their subconscious mind, providing an opportunity to gain a deeper understanding of their thoughts, emotions, and behaviors. For example, meditation may allow individuals to quiet their conscious mind and tune into their inner thoughts and emotions, while hypnosis can allow individuals to access subconscious memories and associations that are not accessible in a waking state.

Overall, the subconscious mind is a complex and multifaceted concept that is still not fully understood by psychologists and neuroscientists. However, it is clear that it plays a critical role in shaping our thoughts, emotions, and behaviors, and that understanding its workings is an important area of study within psychology. The study of the subconscious mind has important implications for improving mental health and well-being, as it provides a way to gain insight into the hidden drivers of our behavior and make changes to promote positive outcomes.

- *Unconscious mind*

The unconscious mind is a key concept in psychology and is often defined as the part of the psyche that is not readily accessible to conscious awareness or introspection. It includes mental processes that are outside of our conscious awareness, such as automatic thoughts, emotions, and behaviors. The unconscious mind is believed to play a critical role in shaping our thoughts, emotions, and behaviors, often in ways that we are not fully aware of.

One of the most influential theories of the unconscious mind is Freud's psychoanalytic theory, which posits that the unconscious mind is the repository of our deepest desires, fears, and motivations. According to Freud, these unconscious drives are often in conflict with one another and with our conscious desires, leading to psychological distress and dysfunction. He believed that by bringing these unconscious drives into conscious awareness through psychoanalysis, individuals could gain insight into their behavior and achieve greater psychological health.

More recent research has focused on the role of the unconscious mind in processing information and influencing behavior. For example, studies have shown that subliminal stimuli, or stimuli that are presented too quickly or faintly to be consciously perceived, can influence subsequent behavior. In one classic study, participants were shown images of either a smiling or frowning face for a few milliseconds, too brief to be consciously perceived. Later, when asked to rate their mood, participants who had been subliminally shown the smiling face reported feeling happier than those who had been shown the frowning face.

Research has also shown that the unconscious mind plays a critical role in regulating emotional responses. For example, studies have shown that when individuals are presented with threatening stimuli, such as a picture of a snake, their amygdala, a brain region involved in fear processing, is activated even if they are not consciously aware of the stimulus. This suggests that the unconscious mind can play a critical role in shaping our emotional responses to the world around us.

In addition to emotions and motivations, the unconscious mind is also believed to play a critical role in memory processing. Research has shown that even when we are not consciously aware of learning something, such as a new skill or a piece of information, it can still be stored and accessed unconsciously. This suggests that the unconscious mind is capable of processing and storing a vast amount of information, often outside of our conscious awareness.

Overall, the unconscious mind is a critical component of our psychological makeup, influencing our thoughts, emotions, and behaviors in ways that we may not even be aware of. While our conscious mind allows us to interact with the world around us and make deliberate choices, the unconscious mind plays a more subtle but no less important role in shaping our experiences and guiding our behavior. Understanding the workings of the unconscious mind is a key area of study within psychology, with implications for everything from psychotherapy to marketing and advertising.

- ***Id***

The id is the most basic and primitive part of our psyche.

It is the source of our instinctual and primal desires, and it seeks immediate gratification without regard for consequences or morality. Here's an example to help illustrate the concept of id:

Imagine you are walking down the street feeling hungry. Suddenly, you see a delicious-looking cake in a bakery window. Your id immediately responds with a strong urge to go into the bakery and eat the cake, regardless of whether it is healthy or whether you have the money to buy it. The id simply wants what it wants, without considering any potential negative consequences.

Another example of the id at work might be the urge to engage in sexual activity without regard for social norms or consequences. The id seeks pleasure and gratification at the moment, and it can sometimes override other considerations such as safety, health, or social conventions.

- *Ego*

The ego is part of the psyche that represents the rational, conscious self, and is responsible for mediating between the id's primitive impulses and the demands of the external world. It operates on the "reality principle," seeking to satisfy the id's desires in a realistic and socially acceptable way.

One example of the ego in action might be a person who is feeling hungry but is also aware that it is not socially acceptable to eat in the middle of a business meeting. The ego would mediate between the person's hunger (which is driven by the id) and the social norms and expectations of the business meeting (which are enforced by the super-ego).

The person might come up with a compromise solution, such as discreetly snacking on a protein bar during a break in the meeting, satisfying their hunger in a way that does not disrupt the social context.

In this example, the ego is operating on the reality principle, finding a solution that satisfies both the id's desire for food and the demands of the external world.

- ***Super-ego***

The super-ego is the component of the psyche that represents the internalized moral standards and values of society. It acts as a kind of conscience, providing a sense of right and wrong and regulating our behavior based on what is considered socially acceptable.

An example of the super-ego in action could be someone who is offered a job that pays very well but is also unethical or illegal. While their id may be tempted by the prospect of money and pleasure, their super-ego would step in to remind them of their moral and ethical obligations. The super-ego might cause them to feel guilty or ashamed of even considering such a job and could ultimately prevent them from accepting it, even if it means passing up a significant financial opportunity.

Another example might be someone who is tempted to cheat on their partner. While their id may be driven by sexual desire and the prospect of pleasure, their super-ego would remind them of the values of loyalty and fidelity that are generally considered important in relationships. The super-ego might cause them to feel guilty or ashamed of even considering such a betrayal and could ultimately prevent them from acting on their impulses, even if it means resisting a strong urge.

3.2 *The Interaction between Id, Ego, and Super-ego*

The interaction between the id, ego, and super-ego is a fundamental concept in psychoanalytic theory, first proposed by Sigmund Freud. According to this theory, the psyche is composed of three distinct parts: the id, ego, and super-ego. Each of these parts represents different aspects of the psyche and has a unique role to play in shaping human behavior and motivation. Let's explore the interaction between the id, ego, and super-ego.

- *Id and ego*

The interaction between the id and ego is an important concept in psychoanalytic theory, developed by Sigmund Freud. The id represents the most primitive and instinctual part of the psyche, consisting of innate drives and impulses that seek immediate gratification. The ego, on the other hand, is the rational and logical part of the psyche, responsible for mediating between the demands of the id and the constraints of reality.

The interaction between the id and ego can be seen as a dynamic tension between two opposing forces. The id is driven by unconscious desires and impulses, seeking immediate pleasure and gratification without regard for the consequences. The ego, on the other hand, is driven by conscious awareness and rational thinking, seeking to find a balance between the demands of the id and the realities of the external world.

In this dynamic tension, the ego acts as a mediator, negotiating between the demands of the id and the constraints of reality. For example, if the id is seeking immediate gratification, the ego may employ rational thinking to delay or redirect that gratification in a way that is more socially acceptable or less harmful. Similarly, if the id is producing anxiety or fear, the ego may work to find ways to reduce that anxiety or fear through rational thinking or problem-solving.

At times, the interaction between the id and ego can result in conflict, with the id pushing for immediate gratification and the ego trying to impose constraints and delay gratification. This can result in a range of psychological symptoms, including anxiety, depression, and compulsive behaviors.

The interaction between the id and ego is important because it provides a framework for understanding the dynamics of human behavior and motivation. By understanding how these two opposing forces interact, we can gain insight into the unconscious processes that drive our behavior and develop strategies for coping with the challenges of everyday life.

Here are two examples of the interaction between the id and ego:

1) *Eating a Delicious Cake*

The id might crave a delicious cake and want to eat the entire thing right away. However, the ego would consider the consequences of such an action, such as potential weight gain, unhealthy eating habits, and possibly feeling guilty. The ego might then negotiate a compromise, allowing the individual to have a smaller portion of the cake or save the cake for a special occasion.

2) *Making a Major Purchase*

The id might desire a luxury item, such as an expensive car or designer handbag, but the ego would consider the practicalities and feasibility of such a purchase, such as whether it fits into the individual's budget, lifestyle, and priorities. The ego might then negotiate a compromise, such as saving up money over time or purchasing a more affordable version of the item.

- ### *Id and super-ego*

The interaction between the id and the super-ego is a crucial aspect of Freud's psychoanalytic theory. According to Freud, the id is the most primitive and instinctual part of the psyche. It is responsible for our most basic drives and desires, such as hunger, thirst, and sexual desire. The id operates on the pleasure principle, seeking immediate gratification of its needs and desires without regard for the consequences or the needs of others.

In contrast, the super-ego represents the internalized moral standards and values of society. It is responsible for our sense of right and wrong, and it functions to keep our more primal desires in check. The super-ego is formed during childhood as we internalize the values, beliefs, and expectations of our parents and other authority figures.

The tension between the id and super-ego arises because these two aspects of the psyche have conflicting goals and desires.

The id seeks immediate gratification and pleasure, while the super-ego seeks to uphold moral principles and social norms. This conflict can lead to feelings of guilt, anxiety, and internal turmoil.

The ego serves as a mediator between the id and super-ego, attempting to balance the conflicting demands of both. The ego operates on the reality principle, seeking to find realistic and socially acceptable ways to satisfy the desires of the id while also adhering to the moral standards of the super-ego. The ego is responsible for decision-making, problem-solving, and the regulation of behavior.

When the ego successfully mediates the tension between the id and super-ego, individuals can behave in socially acceptable ways while still satisfying their basic needs and desires. However, when this balance is disrupted, individuals may experience psychological distress and maladaptive behaviors.

Overall, the interaction between the id and super-ego is a complex process that plays a crucial role in shaping our thoughts, emotions, and behaviors. By understanding these internal conflicts and how the ego mediates them, individuals may be better equipped to navigate the challenges of everyday life and maintain their mental health and well-being.

Here are two examples of the interaction between the id and super-ego:

1) *Cheating on a Test*

The id might be tempted to cheat on a test to get a good grade and achieve a sense of immediate gratification. However, the super-ego would remind the individual of the moral and ethical standards of society, such as honesty and integrity, and discourage them from cheating. The super-ego might also create feelings of guilt and shame if the individual does choose to cheat.

2) *Stealing from a Store*

The id might be tempted to steal something from a store, driven by the desire for material possessions or the thrill of breaking the rules. However, the super-ego would remind the individual of the legal and moral standards of society, such as respect for property rights and the importance of respecting others' property. The super-ego might also create feelings of guilt and shame if the individual does choose to steal.

- ### *Ego and super-ego*

To understand the interaction between the ego and super-ego, it's important to understand the functions of each. The ego is the conscious part of the psyche that mediates between the conflicting demands of the id and the external world. It seeks to satisfy the demands of the id in a way that is socially acceptable and realistic. The super-ego, on the other hand, represents our internalized moral standards and societal values. It provides a sense of morality and conscience and guides us toward making decisions that are in line with our values and ethics.

When there is a conflict between the desires of the id and the moral values of the super-ego, the ego plays a crucial role in negotiating between the two. The ego must balance the demands of the id with the constraints imposed by the super ego, in a way that is socially acceptable and realistic.

For example, imagine a person who is hungry and sees a delicious cake on a table. The id might urge the person to take the cake and eat it, satisfying their immediate desire. However, the super-ego might remind the person of the moral principle that it's wrong to take something that doesn't belong to them. The ego would then need to negotiate between the two conflicting demands, weighing the benefits of satisfying the immediate desire with the moral implications of stealing.

In this negotiation process, the ego may use defense mechanisms such as rationalization or repression to find a compromise between the id and super-ego. Rationalization might involve justifying a decision to satisfy the id's desire by convincing oneself that it's not morally wrong or that there are valid reasons to do so. Repression involves pushing down unacceptable desires or thoughts into the unconscious mind.

Overall, the interaction between the ego and super-ego is a delicate balancing act, requiring the ego to navigate the conflicting demands of our desires and morality. The ego must find a compromise that satisfies our desires while also aligning with our moral principles and societal values.

Here are two examples of the interaction between the ego and super-ego:

1) *Making a Difficult Decision*

Suppose an individual is faced with a difficult decision that requires balancing their desires with their sense of morality. The ego would weigh the options and consider the potential consequences of each choice. The super-ego would then provide a moral perspective, taking into account societal norms and values, and guiding the individual towards a decision that aligns with their moral principles. The ego would then make the final decision, taking into account both the individual's desires and the moral considerations provided by the super-ego.

2) *Balancing Work and Personal Life*

In today's fast-paced world, it can be challenging to balance work and personal life. The id might urge an individual to work long hours to achieve success and financial security. However, the super-ego would remind the individual of the importance of family, friends, and personal relationships, and encourage them to prioritize these relationships over work. The ego would then need to balance the individual's desires for success with their moral obligation to maintain healthy personal relationships. The ego might help the individual to set boundaries and find a balance between work and personal life that aligns with their moral values.

The Development of the Psyche

Overview

65

- ❖ ***The Stages of Psychological development***

  - ✓ *Jean Piaget's Theory of Cognitive Development*
  - ✓ *Lawrence Kohlberg's Theory of Moral Development*
  - ✓ *Lev Vygotsky's Sociocultural Theory*
  - ✓ *Erik Erikson's Psychosocial Development Theory*
  - ✓ *John Bowlby's Attachment Theory*

- ❖ ***Experiences and the development of the Psyche***

- ❖ ***Relationships and the development of the Psyche***

4.1 The Stages of Psychological development

Several famous psychological developmental theories have been proposed by different theorists. Here are some of the most notable:

- ### *Jean Piaget's Theory of Cognitive Development*

Jean Piaget's theory of cognitive development is a comprehensive theory that describes how children learn and develop cognitive abilities from infancy to adolescence. Piaget believed that children actively construct knowledge about the world through their experiences, rather than simply receiving knowledge passively. Piaget's theory proposes four stages of cognitive development:

✓ *Sensorimotor Stage (Birth to 2 years)*

During this stage, infants learn about the world primarily through their senses and actions. They begin to develop object permanence, which is the understanding that objects continue to exist even when they are not visible. Infants also begin to use symbols, such as gestures and words, to represent objects and events in their environment.

✓ *Preoperational Stage (2 to 7 years)*

During this stage, children begin to use language and symbols to represent objects and events in their environment. They also begin to develop more sophisticated mental representations, such as the ability to pretend or imagine things that are not present. However, their thinking is still egocentric, meaning they have difficulty seeing things from another person's perspective.

✓ *Concrete Operational Stage (7 to 11 years)*

During this stage, children become more capable of logical thinking and begin to understand concrete principles of cause and effect. They can also begin to classify objects based on their physical characteristics and use logical thinking to solve problems.

✓ *Formal Operational Stage (11 years and up)*

During this stage, individuals develop the ability to think abstractly and logically. They can also use hypothetical reasoning and deductive reasoning to solve complex problems and understand complex systems.

Piaget's theory has been influential in the field of developmental psychology and has been used to inform educational practices and curriculum development. However, Piaget's theory has also been criticized for placing too much emphasis on the individual's cognitive abilities and not taking into account the role of social and cultural factors in cognitive development.

Here are two supporting examples that illustrate Piaget's theory of cognitive development:

1) *Object Permanence*

According to Piaget's theory, infants develop the ability to understand object permanence during the sensorimotor stage.

One example of this is the classic "peek-a-boo" game. When playing peek-a-boo with a young infant, the caregiver hides their face and then reveals it again, often eliciting laughter and excitement from the infant. This game demonstrates the infant's developing understanding of object permanence, as they begin to realize that the caregiver's face still exists even when it is temporarily hidden from view.

2) *Conservation*

According to Piaget's theory, children in the concrete operational stage can understand principles of conservation, such as the fact that the quantity of a substance remains the same even if it is poured into a different container. One example of this is the classic "tall glass, short glass" experiment. A child is shown two glasses with the same amount of water, and then one glass is poured into a taller, thinner glass. The child is then asked which glass has more water. Children in the preoperational stage might say that the taller glass has more water, while children in the concrete operational stage would understand that the quantity of water remains the same regardless of the glass's shape. This demonstrates their developing ability to use logic and understand abstract principles.

- ### *Lawrence Kohlberg's Theory of Moral Development*

Lawrence Kohlberg's theory of moral development is a psychological theory that proposes that individuals progress through a series of moral stages as they develop. Kohlberg believed that moral development is a continuous process that occurs throughout an individual's lifetime and each stage builds on the preceding one.

According to Kohlberg's theory, there are six stages of moral development that individuals go through, grouped into three levels:

✓ *Level 1: Pre-conventional morality*

Stage 1: Obedience and Punishment Orientation

At this stage, individuals are concerned with avoiding punishment and obedience to authority figures. They believe that what is right is what they are told to do, and what is wrong is what they are forbidden from doing.

Stage 2: Individualism and Exchange

At this stage, individuals are concerned with their interests and the interests of those close to them. They believe that what is right is what satisfies their own needs, and what is wrong is what does not.

✓ *Level 2: Conventional morality*

Stage 3: Interpersonal Relationships

At this stage, individuals are concerned with being good people in the eyes of others. They believe that what is right is what pleases others, and what is wrong is what disappoints them.

Stage 4: Maintaining Social Order

At this stage, individuals are concerned with obeying the laws and upholding the social order. They believe that what is right is what is in the best interests of society, and what is wrong is what goes against it.

✓ *Level 3: Post-conventional morality*

Stage 5: Social Contract and Individual Rights

At this stage, individuals are concerned with protecting individual rights and the well-being of society as a whole. They believe that what is right is what promotes the greatest good for the greatest number of people.

Stage 6: Universal Principles

At this final stage, individuals are concerned with universal ethical principles that apply to all people. They believe that what is right is based on a set of principles that are independent of personal or social context.

It is important to note that not all individuals reach the highest stage of moral development and that some individuals may regress to lower stages under certain circumstances. Kohlberg's theory has been influential in shaping the field of moral psychology and has been used in a variety of applications, including education, law, and psychology.

- ### *Lev Vygotsky's Sociocultural Theory*

Lev Vygotsky's sociocultural theory is a highly influential perspective in developmental psychology that emphasizes the role of social interaction, culture, and language in cognitive development. Vygotsky believed that cognitive development is a result of complex interactions between individuals and their cultural environments, and that language plays a critical role in shaping cognitive development.

Vygotsky's theory is centered on the idea that the development of higher cognitive processes, such as thinking, problem-solving, and decision-making, is influenced by social and cultural factors. According to Vygotsky, individuals acquire these higher cognitive processes through social interactions with more knowledgeable individuals who provide guidance, support, and feedback.

One of the key concepts in Vygotsky's theory is scaffolding, which refers to the process by which a more knowledgeable individual supports a less knowledgeable individual in performing a task. Through scaffolding, the less knowledgeable individual gradually develops their skills and knowledge, eventually becoming capable of performing the task independently.

Another important concept in Vygotsky's theory is the zone of proximal development (ZPD), which refers to the range of tasks that a child can perform with guidance and support from a more knowledgeable individual.

The ZPD is an important concept in educational contexts because it highlights the importance of providing students with tasks that are challenging but achievable with guidance and support.

Vygotsky also emphasized the role of language in cognitive development, proposing that language serves as a critical tool for thinking and problem-solving. According to Vygotsky, language not only reflects an individual's thinking, but it also shapes and guides thinking.

Language allows individuals to communicate their thoughts, ask questions, and receive feedback, which in turn helps to expand their thinking and knowledge.

Finally, Vygotsky's theory highlights the importance of cultural factors in shaping cognitive development. Vygotsky believed that cultural norms, values, and practices influence the way individuals think and interact with the world. Different cultures have different approaches to cognitive development, and cultural differences can have a significant impact on the way individuals learn and develop.

Overall, Vygotsky's sociocultural theory has had a profound impact on the field of developmental psychology and education. It has highlighted the importance of social interaction, culture, and language in cognitive development, and has influenced educational practices around the world.

- ***Erik Erikson's Psychosocial Development Theory***

Erik Erikson's psychosocial development theory is a psychological theory that emphasizes the importance of social and cultural factors in personality development. According to Erikson, personality development occurs through a series of psychosocial stages that span an individual's lifespan. Erikson's theory is based on the idea that individuals go through eight stages of psychosocial development, each of which is characterized by a particular conflict or crisis that must be resolved for healthy personality development to occur.

These stages are:

✓ *Trust vs. Mistrust (infancy)*

During this stage, infants develop a sense of trust or mistrust based on the consistency and predictability of their caregivers' responses to their needs.

✓ *Autonomy vs. Shame and Doubt (toddlerhood)*

During this stage, toddlers develop a sense of autonomy and self-control or may experience shame and doubt if their attempts at independence are discouraged.

✓ *Initiative vs. Guilt (preschool)*

During this stage, preschoolers develop a sense of initiative and purpose or may experience guilt and anxiety if they feel their actions are socially inappropriate.

✓ *Industry vs. Inferiority (school-age)*

During this stage, children develop a sense of competence and accomplishment or may experience feelings of inferiority and inadequacy if they are unable to meet expectations.

✓ *Identity vs. Role Confusion (adolescence)*

During this stage, adolescents develop a sense of identity and who they are or may experience confusion and uncertainty about their identity and role in society.

✓ *Intimacy vs. Isolation (young adulthood)*

During this stage, young adults develop close relationships with others or may experience feelings of isolation and loneliness.

✓ *Generativity vs. Stagnation (middle adulthood)*

During this stage, middle-aged adults focus on contributing to society and future generations or may experience feelings of stagnation and a lack of purpose.

✓ *Ego Integrity vs. Despair (late adulthood)*

During this stage, older adults reflect on their lives and may experience a sense of integrity and fulfillment or despair and regret.

Erikson believed that individuals who successfully resolve the conflicts in each stage develop a healthy sense of self and a positive outlook on life, while those who do not may struggle with identity issues, interpersonal relationships, and a general sense of dissatisfaction with life.

Overall, Erikson's psychosocial development theory has had a significant impact on the field of psychology, particularly in the areas of personality development and lifespan development. It has helped to highlight the importance of social and cultural factors in personality development and has provided a framework for understanding the challenges individuals face at different stages of life.

- ### *John Bowlby's Attachment Theory*

John Bowlby's attachment theory is a psychological theory that emphasizes the importance of early relationships and attachments in shaping an individual's emotional and social development. According to Bowlby, infants, and young children have an innate need to form strong emotional bonds with their primary caregivers, which he referred to as attachment figures.

Bowlby believed that attachment figures provide a secure base from which children can explore and learn about their environment. He proposed that there are four stages of attachment, which are:

✓ *Pre-attachment (birth to 6 weeks)*

During this stage, infants are social beings and seek human contact, but they do not yet form attachments.

✓ *Attachment in the making (6 weeks to 6-8 months)*

During this stage, infants begin to form preferences for specific caregivers, and they become more easily soothed by familiar adults.

✓ ***Clear-cut attachment (6-8 months to 18-24 months)***

During this stage, infants show a clear preference for their primary caregiver, and they become upset when separated from them.

✓ ***Formation of a reciprocal relationship (18-24 months and beyond)***

During this stage, toddlers begin to understand that their attachment figure will return when they are separated, and they use this knowledge to form a more reciprocal and interactive relationship with their caregiver.

Bowlby believed that disruptions to early attachment relationships can have significant and lasting effects on an individual's emotional and social development. He identified three types of attachment styles that can develop based on the quality of the attachment relationship:

✓ ***Secure attachment***

Children with a secure attachment style have caregivers who are responsive and consistent in meeting their needs. They develop a positive self-image and can form healthy relationships with others.

✓ ***Anxious-ambivalent attachment***

Children with an anxious-ambivalent attachment style have caregivers who are inconsistent in meeting their needs. They may become clingy and anxious when separated from their caregiver, and they may have difficulty forming trusting relationships with others.

✓ *Avoidant attachment*

Children with an avoidant attachment style have caregivers who are emotionally distant and unresponsive to their needs. They may become emotionally withdrawn and avoid close relationships with others.

Overall, Bowlby's attachment theory has had a significant impact on the field of developmental psychology and has highlighted the importance of early relationships and attachments in shaping an individual's emotional and social development. It has also informed interventions and therapies aimed at addressing attachment-related issues.

These are just a few of the many notable theories of psychological development that have been proposed by psychologists over the years. Each theory provides a unique perspective on how individuals grow and develop across their lifespans.

4.2 *Experiences and the development of the Psyche*

The psyche, or the human mind, is a complex and multifaceted construct that encompasses both conscious and unconscious aspects. It is shaped and influenced by a range of internal and external factors, including genetic predisposition, environmental influences, cultural and societal norms, and individual experiences.

One of the most important factors that contribute to the

development of the psyche is our experiences. Our experiences shape our perceptions, emotions, thoughts, and behaviors, and play a crucial role in determining how we see ourselves and interact with the world around us.

During childhood, experiences such as attachment, parenting styles, and early socialization can have a profound impact on the development of the psyche. For example, children who have secure attachments with their caregivers tend to develop stronger emotional regulation and self-esteem than those who do not. This is because secure attachment provides a sense of safety and security that enables children to explore the world around them and form healthy relationships with others. Similarly, children who experience consistent and positive parenting styles are more likely to develop healthy coping mechanisms and emotional regulation skills, which can help them manage stress and anxiety later in life.

As we grow and experience more of the world, our experiences continue to shape our psyche. Traumatic experiences, such as abuse or neglect, can have a lasting impact on our mental health and can lead to disorders such as post-traumatic stress disorder (PTSD). This is because traumatic experiences can disrupt our sense of safety and security, leading to feelings of helplessness, anxiety, and depression. Positive experiences, such as relationships, hobbies, and achievements, can contribute to feelings of happiness, satisfaction, and self-worth, which can in turn help us cope with the challenges of daily life.

Overall, the experiences we have throughout our lives contribute to the development of our psyche in a multitude of ways. These experiences can shape our beliefs, values, and attitudes, influencing how we see ourselves and interact with the world around us. Understanding the role of experiences in the development of the psyche is crucial for promoting mental health and well-being, as it enables individuals and professionals to better understand the complex interplay of internal and external factors that contribute to our sense of self and our ability to navigate the world around us.

4.3 Relationships and the development of the Psyche

Human beings are social creatures, and the quality of our relationships can have a profound impact on our psychological development throughout our lives. Relationships with parents and caregivers during childhood are particularly important in shaping the development of the psyche. Infants and young children who experience consistent and nurturing care from their caregivers are more likely to develop secure attachment styles. Secure attachment has been linked to a range of positive outcomes, including emotional regulation, self-esteem, and the ability to form healthy relationships later in life.

On the other hand, children who experience neglect, abuse, or inconsistent care from their caregivers may develop insecure attachment styles. Insecure attachment can lead to a range of negative outcomes, including anxiety, depression, and poor self-esteem. Additionally, children who experience conflict or instability in their family relationships may be at increased risk of developing emotional and behavioral problems.

Throughout adolescence and adulthood, the quality of our romantic relationships can also have a significant impact on our psychological well-being. Positive romantic relationships can provide emotional support, intimacy, and a sense of purpose, while negative or abusive relationships can lead to feelings of anxiety, depression, and poor self-esteem. Additionally, positive relationships with friends, family members, and colleagues can provide a sense of community and social support, contributing to overall mental health and well-being.

Not all relationships are positive, however, and toxic relationships can have a damaging impact on the psyche. Toxic relationships are characterized by abuse, neglect, manipulation, or other harmful behaviors. Individuals who experience toxic relationships may be at increased risk of developing anxiety, depression, and trauma-related symptoms.

Social isolation and loneliness can also harm mental health and well-being. People who lack social connections may be at increased risk of developing depression, anxiety, and other mental health disorders. Social support, on the other hand, has been linked to improved mental health outcomes, including reduced risk of depression and anxiety.

Overall, relationships play a critical role in the development of the psyche throughout the lifespan. Positive relationships can contribute to emotional well-being, while negative or toxic relationships can have a damaging impact on mental health. Understanding the role of relationships in psychological development can help individuals and professionals identify areas for growth and support, promoting mental health and well-being over the lifespan.

Psychological Processes

Overview

❖ **Perception, Attention, and Memory**

- ✓ *What is Perception?*
- ✓ *What is Attention?*
- ✓ *What is Memory?*
- ✓ *The Interaction between Perception, Attention, and Memory*

❖ **Emotions and Motivation**

- ✓ *The Concept of Emotions*
- ✓ *The Concept of Motivation*
- ✓ *The Relationship between Emotions and Motivation*

❖ **Cognitive Biases and Heuristics**

- ✓ *The Concept of Cognitive biases*
- ✓ *The Concept of Heuristics*
- ✓ *The Relationship between Cognitive biases and Heuristics*

5.1 Perception, Attention, and Memory

Perception, attention, and memory are interconnected cognitive processes that play a crucial role in how we understand and interact with the world around us.

- ### *What is Perception?*

Perception is a complex and multifaceted process that involves the interpretation and integration of sensory information from our environment. Sensory information can be received through various modalities such as sight, sound, touch, taste, and smell. The process of perception begins when our sensory receptors detect environmental stimuli and send signals to our brains. These signals are then transformed into neural impulses that are processed and interpreted by the brain.

One key aspect of perception is that it is influenced by our past experiences, expectations, and beliefs. Our brain uses these pre-existing schemas to help interpret incoming sensory information. For example, if we have had positive experiences with dogs in the past, we may perceive a dog barking as friendly, while someone who has had negative experiences with dogs may perceive the same barking as threatening. Similarly, if we expect to see something in our environment, we may be more likely to perceive it, even if it is not there.

Another factor that influences perception is attention. Our brains have limited processing capacity, so we must selectively attend to the most important stimuli in our environment. Our attention can be influenced by both bottom-up factors (such as the physical characteristics of a stimulus) and top-down factors (such as our goals or expectations). For example, if we are looking for our friend in a crowded room, we may selectively attend to stimuli that are similar to our friend's appearance or behavior.

Memory also plays a crucial role in perception. Our past experiences and knowledge are stored in our long-term memory and can influence how we interpret incoming sensory information. For example, if we have learned that a certain shape or color is associated with a particular object, we may be more likely to perceive that object when we encounter stimuli with those same characteristics.

- ***What is Attention?***

Attention is a cognitive process that allows us to selectively process and focus on specific aspects of our environment while ignoring other stimuli. It is a critical mechanism that enables us to efficiently process and organize sensory information from our surroundings. Attention allows us to filter out irrelevant or distracting stimuli and to concentrate on the essential aspects of a given situation or task. It is an essential component of perception, cognition, and behavior, and it plays a critical role in our everyday lives.

At its most basic level, attention involves the ability to focus one's cognitive resources on a particular stimulus or task. This process requires the allocation of cognitive resources, such as attentional capacity, processing speed, and working memory, to the task at hand. The allocation of these resources is flexible, allowing individuals to adjust their focus as needed and to switch attentional focus from one stimulus to another.

The process of attention can be divided into several distinct stages, including selective attention, divided attention sustained attention and executive attention. Selective attention involves the ability to focus on specific stimuli while ignoring other distractors. Divided attention involves the ability to process multiple stimuli simultaneously. Sustained attention refers to the ability to maintain focus over an extended period, and executive attention involves the ability to inhibit automatic responses and to flexibly adjust attentional focus as needed.

Attention is closely linked to perception, as it can influence how we perceive and interpret sensory information. For example, selective attention can lead us to focus on one particular aspect of a scene or object, leading to biases in perception. Attention can also influence the salience of stimuli, with more salient stimuli being more likely to capture our attention.

Additionally, attentional mechanisms are involved in the processing of emotional information, with emotional stimuli often capturing our attention more quickly and strongly than non-emotional stimuli.

Finally, attention is also closely linked to cognition and behavior, with attentional deficits being associated with a range of cognitive and behavioral problems. For example, individuals with attention deficit hyperactivity disorder (ADHD) may experience difficulties with sustained attention, while individuals with anxiety disorders may experience difficulties with selective attention. Attentional deficits can also lead to problems with memory, decision-making, and problem-solving.

• *What is Memory?*

Memory is a complex and multi-stage process that involves the encoding, storage, and retrieval of information from our past experiences. Encoding refers to the initial process of converting information from sensory inputs into a form that can be processed and stored in the brain. This involves the selection and manipulation of information from the environment through the senses, such as sight, sound, taste, touch, and smell. The brain then integrates this information with prior knowledge and existing memories to create a meaningful representation of the experience.

Storage refers to the process of maintaining and consolidating the encoded information over time. The brain has various regions and systems that are responsible for storing different types of information, such as short-term memory, long-term memory, and working memory. Short-term memory is a temporary storage that can hold a limited amount of information for a few seconds to a few minutes. Working memory is a system that allows us to manipulate and process information in our minds while we are performing a task. Long-term memory is the relatively permanent store that holds information for hours, days, months, or even years. It is thought to involve the strengthening and modification of connections between neurons in the brain.

Retrieval refers to the process of accessing and retrieving stored information from memory. This involves the activation of neural circuits that were formed during encoding and storage. Retrieval can be influenced by various factors, such as the strength of the original memory, the similarity between the retrieval cue and the stored information, and the context in which the memory was encoded and stored. Retrieval can also be improved through practice and repetition.

Memory is crucial for learning and decision-making, as it allows us to retain and access information that we have acquired over time. Memory also plays a key role in shaping our perceptions and attention. Our memories can influence our perceptions, as our expectations and prior knowledge can bias how we interpret and process new information. For example, if we have a strong memory of a positive experience with a certain type of food, we may be more likely to perceive it as delicious in the future. Our attention can also influence the information that we encode and store in our memory. If we pay more attention to certain aspects of an experience, we may be more likely to remember them later on.

Overall, memory is a complex and dynamic process that plays a crucial role in our daily lives. By understanding the different stages of memory and the factors that influence it, we can improve our ability to learn, remember, and make decisions based on our past experiences.

In summary, perception, attention, and memory are three interconnected cognitive processes that work together to help us make sense of the world around us. Our perceptions shape our attention, our attention shapes our memory, and our memory influences our perceptions, creating a continuous cycle of cognitive processing.

- ***The Interaction between Perception, Attention, and Memory***

Perception, attention, and memory are three closely related cognitive processes that work together to help us process, store, and recall information from our environment. Here's how they interact:

1) *Perception and Attention*

Perception and attention are closely intertwined because attention helps us to select and focus on certain sensory information, while perception allows us to interpret that information. For example, if you're in a noisy room, your attention might focus on the person you're talking to, while your perception helps you to understand what they're saying despite the background noise.

Selective attention plays an important role in perception. When we selectively attend to certain aspects of our environment, we are more likely to perceive them. For example, if we are looking for a specific object in a cluttered environment, we are more likely to perceive it if we selectively attend to the relevant features.

Additionally, perception can influence attention. If we perceive a stimulus as important or salient, we are more likely to attend to it. For example, if we see a bright flashing light, we are more likely to attend to it than to other stimuli in the environment.

2) *Attention and Memory*

Attention is the ability to focus on certain aspects of the environment while ignoring others. It is essential for the formation and retrieval of memories because we can only remember information that we have attended to. In other words, if we don't pay attention to something, we're unlikely to remember it.

Encoding: Attention helps to transfer information into memory by encoding it, or giving it meaning and context. When we pay attention to something, we are more likely to encode it into memory because we are actively processing and engaging with the information.

For example, if you are studying for a test, you need to pay attention to the material to remember it later. If you are distracted or not paying attention, the information is less likely to be encoded into memory.

Additionally, attention can help to prioritize information for encoding. We can only encode a limited amount of information into memory at a time, so attention helps us to select and focus on the most important or relevant information.

Storage: Once the information has been encoded, it is stored in memory. The way we attend to information can impact how it is stored in memory. For example, if we attend to the details of an event, we are more likely to remember specific details later. On the other hand, if we attend to the overall impression of an event, we may be more likely to remember the general gist or theme.

Retrieval: Attention also plays a role in the retrieval of memories. When we retrieve information from memory, we need to attend to the cues or prompts that trigger the memory. For example, if someone mentions a movie you saw last week, you need to attend to that cue to retrieve the memory of the movie.

3) *Perception and Memory*

Perception is the process by which we interpret sensory information from the environment, and it plays a critical role in the formation and retrieval of memories. The way we perceive and interpret information affects how we encode, store, and retrieve memories.

Encoding: Encoding is the process of taking information and transforming it into a format that can be stored in memory. The way we perceive and interpret information can impact how we encode that information. For example, if you are trying to remember a person's face, your perception of their features will affect how you encode that information. If you perceive their features as distinctive or unusual, you are more likely to encode them into memory. On the other hand, if you perceive their features as common or unremarkable, you may be less likely to encode them into memory.

Storage: Once the information has been encoded, it is stored in memory. The way we perceive and interpret information can also impact how we store memories. For example, memories that are associated with strong emotions or are meaningful to us are more likely to be stored in long-term memory. Similarly, memories that are associated with multiple sensory cues (such as sight, sound, and smell) are more likely to be stored in memory. This is because multiple cues provide more pathways for retrieval, making the memory easier to access later.

Retrieval: Retrieval is the process of accessing information that has been stored in memory. Perception plays a crucial role in retrieval by providing contextual cues that can trigger memories. For example, if you smell a particular scent, it may trigger a memory of a previous experience associated with that scent. This is because the scent provides a strong sensory cue that is associated with memory.

Similarly, if you see a familiar face, your perception of their features can trigger a memory of their name or other information associated with them. This is because your perception of their features serves as a contextual cue that can help you retrieve the associated information from memory.

In summary, perception, attention, and memory are all interconnected cognitive processes that work together to help us process, store, and recall information from our environment. Perception allows us to gather sensory information, attention helps us to focus on relevant information and transfer it into memory, and memory allows us to store and retrieve the information later.

5.2 Emotions and Motivation

Emotions and motivation are two important psychological concepts that are closely related. Emotions refer to complex psychological states that involve physiological, subjective, and behavioral responses to stimuli. Motivation refers to the driving force or reason behind the behavior, which can be influenced by emotions.

- ### The Concept of Emotions

Emotions are complex psychological states that are characterized by a range of subjective experiences, physiological responses, and behavioral expressions.

Emotions can be triggered by a variety of internal and external stimuli, including our thoughts, memories, and perceptions of the world around us. Emotions can be short-lived and intense, or they can be more prolonged and less intense, depending on the situation and individual factors.

Positive emotions such as happiness, joy, and contentment are often associated with feelings of well-being, pleasure, and satisfaction. Positive emotions can be triggered by a wide range of events, including successes, accomplishments, and positive interactions with others. They can also be the result of engaging in activities that are meaningful and enjoyable, such as hobbies or spending time with loved ones.

Negative emotions such as anger, fear, and sadness are often associated with feelings of discomfort, distress, and unpleasantness. Negative emotions can be triggered by a range of events, including failures, disappointments, and negative interactions with others. They can also be the result of external factors such as stress, illness, or trauma.

The physiological responses that are associated with emotions can include changes in heart rate, breathing, and skin temperature. These responses are regulated by the autonomic nervous system, which is responsible for controlling involuntary bodily functions. Emotions can also be associated with changes in hormone levels, which can influence mood and behavior.

Behavioral responses to emotions can include facial expressions, body language, and verbal expressions. For example, someone who is feeling happy might smile, laugh, or engage in playful behavior. Someone who is feeling sad might frown, cry, or withdraw from social interactions.

These behavioral expressions can communicate our emotional states to others and can influence the way that others respond to us.

Emotions can influence behavior in a variety of ways, depending on the type of emotion and the specific situation. Positive emotions can increase motivation, creativity, and social engagement, while negative emotions can lead to withdrawal, aggression, and avoidance. Emotions can also influence decision-making, memory, and attention, shaping the way that we interpret and respond to the world around us.

• *The Concept of Motivation*

Motivation is a critical factor in human behavior, as it is what drives us to act and achieve our goals. Motivation can be influenced by a variety of factors, both internal and external.

Internal factors that influence motivation include biological needs, personal goals and values, and the desire for personal growth and self-improvement. For example, hunger and thirst are powerful biological motivators that drive us to seek out food and water. Personal goals, such as completing a project or learning a new skill, can also be strong motivators that help us to focus our attention and energy.

External factors that influence motivation include social and cultural norms, rewards and punishments, and the expectations of others. For example, social and cultural norms can influence our behavior by shaping our beliefs and values about what is important and acceptable in our society. Rewards and punishments, such as praise or criticism from others, can also have a significant impact on our motivation.

Intrinsic motivation is a type of motivation that comes from within, driven by internal factors such as curiosity, enjoyment, and personal growth. Intrinsic motivation is often linked to activities that we find inherently interesting or enjoyable, such as playing a musical instrument or solving a challenging puzzle. Because intrinsic motivation is based on personal interest and enjoyment, it can be a powerful force that drives us to persist and excel in our chosen activities.

Extrinsic motivation, on the other hand, comes from external factors such as rewards, recognition, and punishment. Extrinsic motivation is often used to motivate behavior that might not be inherently interesting or enjoyable, such as completing a tedious task at work. Extrinsic motivation can be effective in the short-term, but it may not be sustainable over the long-term if the rewards or punishments are removed.

Motivation can influence behavior in a variety of ways, depending on the type of motivation and the specific situation. For example, if someone is highly motivated to achieve a goal, they may work harder and persist longer to reach that goal. However, if someone lacks motivation, they may struggle to initiate or sustain behavior, leading to poor performance or failure to achieve their goals.

- ### *The Relationship between Emotions and Motivation*

Emotions and motivation are intertwined and can have a significant impact on each other. Emotions can affect motivation in several ways. For example, positive emotions like happiness, excitement, and enthusiasm can increase intrinsic motivation. Intrinsic motivation is the desire to perform a task for its own sake, rather than for an external reward. When individuals experience positive emotions, they tend to feel more engaged and interested in what they are doing, which can increase their intrinsic motivation to continue the behavior.

On the other hand, negative emotions like fear, anxiety, and stress can decrease motivation. When individuals experience negative emotions, they tend to feel less interested and engaged in what they are doing, which can decrease their intrinsic motivation to continue the behavior. For example, if someone is working on a project and feels overwhelmed by stress and anxiety, they may be less motivated to continue working on the project and may even give up altogether.

Emotions can also influence extrinsic motivation, which is the motivation to perform a task to earn a reward or avoid punishment. For example, if someone receives positive feedback or a reward for a behavior, they may feel happy and motivated to continue the behavior to receive more rewards. Conversely, if someone receives negative feedback or is punished for a behavior, they may feel fear or anxiety and be less motivated to engage in that behavior in the future.

Moreover, the relationship between emotions and motivation is bidirectional. Motivation can also influence emotions. For example, when individuals are motivated to achieve a goal, they may feel a sense of excitement, enthusiasm, and pride when they succeed, which can lead to positive emotions. Similarly, when individuals fail to achieve a goal, they may feel disappointed, frustrated, and sad, which can lead to negative emotions.

In summary, emotions, and motivation are closely related and can have a significant impact on each other. Positive emotions can increase intrinsic motivation, while negative emotions can decrease motivation. Emotions can also influence extrinsic motivation, and motivation can influence emotions. Understanding the relationship between emotions and motivation can help individuals to manage their emotions and increase their motivation to achieve their goals.

5.3 Cognitive Biases and Heuristics

Cognitive biases and heuristics are psychological processes that can impact how we make decisions and judgments. Let's explore them individually:

- **The Concept of Cognitive biases**

Cognitive biases refer to systematic errors in thinking or decision-making that can lead to distorted or irrational judgments. These biases are the result of the brain's natural tendency to take shortcuts in processing information and making decisions, which can sometimes lead to flawed conclusions.

There are many different types of cognitive biases, each with its unique characteristics and effects on decision-making. Some of the most common types of cognitive biases include:

Confirmation Bias: The tendency to look for and interpret information in a way that confirms one's pre-existing beliefs or hypotheses, while ignoring or discounting contradictory evidence.

Anchoring Bias: The tendency to rely too heavily on the first piece of information encountered when making a decision, even if it is not particularly relevant or accurate.

Availability Heuristic: The tendency to overestimate the likelihood of events based on how easily examples come to mind, rather than on actual statistical probabilities.

Halo Effect: The tendency to judge someone or something based on one particular trait or characteristic, rather than looking at the whole picture.

Framing Effect: The tendency for people's judgments or decisions to be influenced by the way information is presented, such as in a positive or negative light.

Overconfidence Bias: The tendency to overestimate one's abilities or knowledge, leading to unrealistic expectations and potentially risky decisions.

Sunk Cost Fallacy: The tendency to continue investing time or resources into a project or decision even if it is no longer a rational choice, because of the sunk costs already incurred.

Bandwagon Effect: The tendency to conform to the opinions or actions of a group, even if they are not aligned with one's personal beliefs or values.

Hindsight Bias: The tendency to believe that an event was predictable after it has already occurred, leading to overconfidence in future predictions.

Negativity Bias: The tendency to give greater weight to negative experiences or information than to positive ones, leading to a more pessimistic outlook.

While cognitive biases are a natural part of the human thought process, they can have negative consequences when they lead to flawed decision-making. By becoming aware of these biases and actively working to mitigate their effects, individuals can make more rational and informed choices. This can be particularly important in fields such as finance, healthcare, and politics, where decisions can have significant consequences.

- ### *The Concept of Heuristics*

Heuristics are mental shortcuts or rules of thumb that people use to make judgments or decisions more quickly and efficiently. Heuristics can be helpful in situations where there is a lot of information to process, or when making a quick decision is necessary. However, heuristics can also lead to errors in judgment or decision-making, especially in complex or unfamiliar situations.

There are many different types of heuristics, but some of the most common include:

Availability Heuristic: The tendency to estimate the likelihood of an event based on how easily examples come to mind. For example, people may overestimate the likelihood of a plane crash after seeing news reports about one, even though flying is statistically much safer than driving.

Representativeness Heuristic: The tendency to judge the likelihood of an event based on how well it matches our mental image or prototype of that event. For example, people may assume that a CEO is more likely to be a man than a woman because their mental image of a CEO is more masculine.

Anchoring Heuristic: The tendency to rely too heavily on the first piece of information encountered when making a decision. For example, people may be more likely to buy a car if the initial price is higher, even if the price is negotiable.

Recognition Heuristic: The tendency to make judgments based on whether something is familiar or recognized. For example, people may be more likely to vote for a political candidate whose name they recognize, even if they do not know anything about their policies or positions.

Framing Heuristic: The tendency for people's judgments or decisions to be influenced by the way information is presented, such as in a positive or negative light. For example, people may be more likely to buy a product if it is presented as a discount or sale, even if the original price was inflated.

Heuristics can be useful in many situations, but they can also lead to errors in judgment or decision-making.

For example, relying too heavily on the availability heuristic can lead to overestimating the likelihood of rare events, such as plane crashes or terrorist attacks. Similarly, relying too heavily on the representativeness heuristic can lead to stereotyping or prejudice.

One way to mitigate the effects of heuristics is to use deliberate, analytical thinking to double-check initial judgments or decisions. This can help to identify and correct any errors or biases that may be present.

Additionally, being aware of the existence of heuristics and their potential effects can help people to make more informed and rational decisions.

- ### *The Relationship between Cognitive biases and heuristics*

Many cognitive biases are related to heuristics. For example, the availability heuristic is a cognitive bias that leads people to estimate the likelihood of an event based on how easily examples come to mind. This bias is related to the availability heuristic, which is a mental shortcut that people use to make judgments based on the information that is most readily available to them.

Similarly, the representativeness heuristic is a mental shortcut that leads people to judge the likelihood of an event based on how well it matches their mental image or prototype of that event. This heuristic is related to the representativeness bias, which is a cognitive bias that leads people to make judgments based on whether something fits their mental image or stereotype of that thing.

Other cognitive biases and heuristics are also closely related. For example, the framing effect is a cognitive bias that leads people's judgments or decisions to be influenced by the way information is presented, such as in a positive or negative light. This bias is related to the framing heuristic, which is a mental shortcut that people use to make judgments based on the way information is presented.

Overall, cognitive biases and heuristics are closely related concepts that can influence the way people make judgments and decisions. By being aware of these biases and heuristics, individuals can make more informed and rational decisions. Additionally, using deliberate, analytical thinking to double-check initial judgments or decisions can help to mitigate the effects of these biases and heuristics.

Personality and the Psyche

Overview

❖ **The Relationship between Personality and the Psyche**

❖ **The different Theories of Personality**

✓ *Psychodynamic theory*
✓ *Humanistic theory*
✓ *Trait theory*
✓ *Biological theory*
✓ *Social-cognitive theory*
✓ *Behavioral theory*
✓ *Cultural theory*

6.1 The Relationship between Personality and the Psyche

The relationship between personality and the psyche is a complex and multifaceted one, and different theoretical perspectives offer different ways of understanding this relationship.

One of the most influential theories of personality and the psyche is psychodynamic theory, which was developed by Sigmund Freud and his followers. According to this theory, personality arises from the interaction between conscious and unconscious elements of the psyche. The psyche is composed of three levels: the conscious mind, the preconscious mind, and the unconscious mind. The conscious mind contains thoughts, feelings, and perceptions that are currently in awareness, while the preconscious mind contains information that is not currently conscious but can be easily retrieved. The unconscious mind is the most important in shaping personality, as it contains repressed memories, desires, and impulses that can exert a powerful influence on conscious behavior.

Freud proposed that the psyche is structured into three components: the id, the ego, and the superego. The id is the primitive and instinctual part of the psyche, which seeks pleasure and avoids pain. The ego is the rational part of the psyche, which mediates between the demands of the id and the constraints of the external world. The superego is the moral and ethical part of the psyche, which represents the internalized values and standards of society.

According to psychodynamic theory, conflicts between the id, ego, and superego can lead to psychological distress and personality disorders. Defense mechanisms, such as repression, projection, and denial, are used by the ego to protect the individual from anxiety and to maintain a stable sense of self.

Another influential theory of personality and the psyche is a humanistic theory, which emphasizes the importance of conscious self-awareness and personal growth in shaping personality. Humanistic theorists, such as Abraham Maslow and Carl Rogers, believe that individuals have an innate drive to achieve self-actualization or the realization of their full potential. According to this theory, the psyche is not seen as a repository of repressed desires and impulses, but rather as a source of creative and meaningful expression.

Humanistic theorists also emphasize the importance of unconditional positive regard or acceptance and support for the individual without judgment or evaluation. This creates a safe and supportive environment that allows the individual to explore and express their true self, leading to greater self-awareness and personal growth.

Trait theory, another approach to personality, focuses on identifying and measuring stable traits or characteristics that are unique to each individual. In this approach, the psyche is seen as a set of underlying traits that determine behavior, thoughts, and emotions. Trait theorists, such as Gordon Allport and Raymond Cattell, have identified a wide range of personality traits, such as extraversion, neuroticism, openness to experience, and conscientiousness.

Trait theory emphasizes the stability of personality traits over time and across situations, suggesting that they have a strong biological and genetic basis. However, some trait theorists also acknowledge the role of environmental factors in shaping personalities, such as cultural norms and socialization processes.

In conclusion, the relationship between personality and the psyche is a complex and multifaceted one, and different theoretical perspectives offer different ways of understanding this relationship. The psychodynamic theory emphasizes the role of unconscious processes and early childhood experiences, while humanistic theory emphasizes conscious self-awareness and personal growth. Trait theory focuses on stable personality traits while acknowledging the role of environmental factors. Overall, these different approaches contribute to our understanding of the dynamic and unique nature of human personality.

6.2 *The different Theories of Personality*

There are many different theories of personality, each of which proposes a unique way of understanding and explaining human personality. Here are some of the major theories of personality:

- *Psychodynamic theory*

Psychodynamic theory is a theoretical perspective that emphasizes the role of unconscious processes and early childhood experiences in shaping personality and behavior. The theory was developed by Sigmund Freud and his followers, and it has been influential in psychology and psychotherapy for over a century.

According to psychodynamic theory, the human psyche is composed of three levels: the conscious mind, the preconscious mind, and the unconscious mind. The conscious mind contains thoughts, feelings, and perceptions that are currently in awareness, while the preconscious mind contains information that is not currently conscious but can be easily retrieved. The unconscious mind is the most important in shaping personality, as it contains repressed memories, desires, and impulses that can exert a powerful influence on conscious behavior.

Freud proposed that the psyche is structured into three components: the id, the ego, and the superego. The id is the primitive and instinctual part of the psyche, which seeks pleasure and avoids pain. The ego is the rational part of the psyche, which mediates between the demands of the id and the constraints of the external world. The superego is the moral and ethical part of the psyche, which represents the internalized values and standards of society.

Conflicts between the id, ego, and superego can lead to psychological distress and personality disorders. Defense mechanisms, such as repression, projection, and denial, are used by the ego to protect the individual from anxiety and to maintain a stable sense of self. Two good examples of psychodynamic theory in action are:

1) *Psychoanalysis:* Psychoanalysis is a form of talk therapy that was developed by Freud. It is based on the idea that many of our problems stem from unconscious conflicts and repressed memories. Through the use of free association, dream analysis, and other techniques, psychoanalysts help clients to uncover these unconscious processes and to work through them in a safe and

supportive environment.

2) ***Attachment theory:*** Attachment theory, developed by John Bowlby and Mary Ainsworth, is based on the idea that early experiences with attachment figures (typically parents or caregivers) shape our patterns of attachment and our approach to relationships throughout life. According to attachment theory, secure attachment is characterized by a sense of safety and trust, while insecure attachment is characterized by anxiety, avoidance, or ambivalence. Attachment theory has been used to explain a wide range of phenomena, from childhood development to adult romantic relationships.

- ***Humanistic theory***

Humanistic theory is a theoretical perspective that emphasizes the importance of subjective experience and personal growth in shaping personality and behavior. This theory emerged in the mid-20th century as a reaction to the more deterministic and behavioristic approaches that dominated psychology at the time.

The humanistic theory focuses on the inherent goodness and potential for growth within individuals and emphasizes the importance of personal choice and responsibility in shaping behavior.

According to humanistic theory, humans have an innate drive towards self-actualization, which is the process of realizing one's full potential and becoming the best version of oneself. This drive toward self-actualization can be hindered by various factors, including societal expectations, negative experiences, and a lack of supportive environments.

Two key concepts within humanistic theory are self-concept and self-esteem. Self-concept refers to the beliefs and attitudes that individuals have about themselves, while self-esteem refers to the emotional evaluation of one's self-concept.

Individuals with a positive self-concept and high self-esteem are more likely to pursue self-actualization and to feel fulfilled in their lives. Two good examples of humanistic theory in action are:

1) ***Person-centered therapy:*** Person-centered therapy, developed by Carl Rogers, is a form of talk therapy that emphasizes empathy, unconditional positive regard, and genuineness in the therapeutic relationship. The goal of this therapy is to help individuals to develop a more positive self-concept and to become more self-actualized.

2) ***Maslow's hierarchy of needs:*** Abraham Maslow proposed a hierarchy of human needs that must be met for individuals to pursue self-actualization. The hierarchy consists of five levels: physiological needs, safety needs, love and belonging needs, esteem needs, and self-actualization needs. According to Maslow, individuals must have their lower-level needs met before they can pursue higher-level needs and achieve self-actualization.

- ***Trait theory***

Trait theory is a theoretical perspective that emphasizes the importance of individual personality differences. This theory assumes that personality can be described in terms of a set of stable, enduring traits or characteristics that vary in degree across individuals. Trait theory suggests that these traits are relatively stable over time and across situations and can predict behavior and outcomes.

According to trait theory, personality can be conceptualized as a set of traits or dimensions that can be measured using self-report questionnaires or other rating scales. Trait theorists identify a set of basic dimensions of personality, such as extraversion, agreeableness, conscientiousness, neuroticism, and openness to experience. These traits are thought to be universal, meaning they are present in all individuals, regardless of culture or ethnicity.

Two key concepts within trait theory are consistency and stability. Consistency refers to the idea that an individual's personality traits are relatively stable across situations and over time. Stability refers to the idea that an individual's personality traits are consistent across the lifespan. Two good examples of trait theory in action are:

1) ***The Big Five model of personality:*** The Big Five model is a widely-used framework for describing personality in terms of five broad dimensions: extraversion, agreeableness, conscientiousness, neuroticism, and openness to experience. These dimensions are relatively stable across cultures and have been associated with a wide range of outcomes, from job performance to health and well-being.

2) ***The Myers-Briggs Type Indicator:*** The Myers-Briggs Type Indicator (MBTI) is a self-report questionnaire that assesses personality across four dimensions:

Extraversion / introversion, sensing / intuition, thinking / feeling, and judging / perceiving. The MBTI is commonly used in organizational settings to help individuals and teams understand their strengths and weaknesses and to improve communication and collaboration.

- ### *Biological theory*

The biological theory is a theoretical perspective that emphasizes the biological and physiological factors that influence personality and behavior. This theory suggests that individual personality differences are partially determined by genetic, hormonal, and neurological factors.

According to biological theory, the structure and function of the brain, as well as the presence of certain genes and hormones, can influence an individual's temperament, behavior, and emotions. This theory also suggests that environmental factors, such as stress or nutrition, can interact with biological factors to shape personality.

Two key concepts within biological theory are heritability and brain structure. Heritability refers to the extent to which individual personality differences are influenced by genetic factors. Brain structure refers to the physical organization of the brain and the specific areas that are responsible for different aspects of personality and behavior. Two good examples of biological theory in action are:

1) *Behavioral genetics:* Behavioral genetics is a field of research that examines the extent to which genetic and environmental factors contribute to individual differences in personality and behavior. This research has found that

many personality traits, such as extraversion and neuroticism, are partially heritable, and certain genes are associated with specific personality traits.

2) Neuroimaging studies: Neuroimaging studies use brain imaging techniques, such as magnetic resonance imaging (MRI), to investigate the neural mechanisms underlying personality and behavior. These studies have found that certain brain regions, such as the prefrontal cortex, are associated with specific personality traits and that differences in brain structure and function can explain individual differences in personality and behavior.

- ***Social-cognitive theory***

The social-cognitive theory is a theoretical perspective that emphasizes the role of both environmental and cognitive factors in shaping personality and behavior.

This theory suggests that individuals learn new behaviors and attitudes by observing and imitating others and that their cognitive processes, such as beliefs and expectations, can also influence their behavior.

According to social-cognitive theory, individuals can learn new behaviors and attitudes by observing others and their consequences, a process known as observational learning or modeling.

This theory also suggests that individuals can regulate their behavior by setting goals, monitoring their progress, and making adjustments as needed.

Two key concepts within social-cognitive theory are self-efficacy and locus of control. Self-efficacy refers to an individual's belief in their ability to perform a task or achieve a goal. Locus of control refers to an individual's belief in the extent to which they have control over their life outcomes. Two good examples of social-cognitive theory in action are:

1) ***Bandura's social learning theory:*** Bandura's social learning theory emphasizes the role of observation and modeling in learning new behaviors and attitudes. This theory suggests that individuals can acquire new behaviors by observing others and their consequences and that they can regulate their behavior by setting goals and monitoring their progress.

2) ***Rotter's social learning theory:*** Rotter's social learning theory emphasizes the role of beliefs and expectations in shaping behavior. This theory suggests that individuals' beliefs about the extent to which they have control over their life outcomes can influence their behavior and well-being.

- ***Behavioral theory***

Behavioral theory is a theoretical perspective that emphasizes the role of environmental factors in shaping personality and behavior. This theory suggests that individuals learn new behaviors through the processes of classical conditioning, operant conditioning, and observational learning.

Classical conditioning is the process by which an individual learns to associate a neutral stimulus with a stimulus that elicits a response, leading to a conditioned response to the neutral stimulus.

Operant conditioning is the process by which an individual learns to associate a behavior with a consequence, leading to an increase or decrease in the frequency of that behavior.

Observational learning is the process by which an individual learns new behaviors by observing and imitating others.

Two key concepts within behavioral theory are reinforcement and punishment. Reinforcement refers to the process of increasing the likelihood of a behavior by providing a positive consequence, such as praise or reward.

Punishment refers to the process of decreasing the likelihood of a behavior by providing a negative consequence, such as criticism or penalty. Two good examples of behavioral theory in action are:

1) ***Skinner's operant conditioning theory:*** Skinner's operant conditioning theory emphasizes the role of reinforcement and punishment in shaping behavior. This theory suggests that individuals learn new behaviors by associating them with positive or negative consequences and that reinforcement is a more effective way to change behavior than punishment.

2) ***Watson's classical conditioning theory:*** Watson's classical conditioning theory emphasizes the role of environmental stimuli in shaping behavior. This theory suggests that individuals learn new behaviors by associating neutral stimuli with stimuli that elicit a response, and that this process can be used to condition

new behaviors.

- ### *Cultural theory*

Cultural theory is a theoretical perspective that emphasizes the role of culture in shaping personality and behavior. This theory suggests that culture provides individuals with a set of shared values, beliefs, and norms that guide their behavior, and that individuals are socialized into their culture through the process of enculturation.

Two key concepts within cultural theory are individualism and collectivism. Individualism refers to a cultural orientation that values independence, autonomy, and self-expression. Collectivism refers to a cultural orientation that values interdependence, cooperation, and social harmony. Two good examples of cultural theory in action are:

1) *Hofstede's cultural dimensions theory:* Hofstede's cultural dimensions theory identifies six dimensions of culture that influence behavior and values, including individualism-collectivism, power distance, uncertainty avoidance, masculinity-femininity, long-term orientation, and indulgence-restraint. This theory suggests that cultural values and norms vary across cultures and can influence behavior and attitudes.

2) *Triandis' theory of individualism and collectivism:* Triandis' theory of individualism and collectivism suggests that culture shapes individuals' self-concepts and values. This theory proposes that individuals from individualistic cultures tend to have a more independent

self-concept and value individual achievement, whereas individuals from collectivistic cultures tend to have a more interdependent self-concept and value social relationships and group harmony.

These are just some of the major theories of personality, and there are many other theories and approaches as well. Each theory offers a unique perspective on the complex and multifaceted nature of human personality.

Mental Health and the Psyche

Overview

❖ **Mental Health disorders and their Impact on the Psyche**

  ✓ *Altering mood and emotions*
  ✓ *Distorting perceptions*
  ✓ *Impairing cognitive functioning*
  ✓ *Affecting behavior and motivation*
  ✓ *Affecting physical health*

❖ **The role of Psychotherapy in Treating Mental health disorders**

  ✓ *Cognitive-behavioral therapy (CBT)*
  ✓ *Psychodynamic therapy*
  ✓ *Interpersonal therapy*
  ✓ *Mindfulness-based therapy*

7.1 Mental Health disorders and their Impact on the Psyche

Mental health disorders can have a significant impact on the psyche or the mental and emotional processes that shape a person's behavior, thoughts, and feelings. The effects of mental health disorders on the psyche can vary depending on the specific disorder, severity, and duration of symptoms. Some common ways mental health disorders can impact the psyche include:

- ***Altering mood and emotions***

Mental health disorders can have a profound impact on an individual's overall well-being and quality of life. These disorders can cause a wide range of emotional and behavioral changes that can be difficult to cope with and manage.

Depression, for example, is a mental health disorder characterized by persistent feelings of sadness, hopelessness, and emptiness. People with depression often experience a loss of interest in activities they once enjoyed and may struggle to find joy or pleasure in anything. They may also have trouble sleeping, eating, and concentrating, and may feel fatigued or sluggish.

Anxiety disorders, on the other hand, can cause feelings of worry, fear, and nervousness that can be overwhelming and interfere with daily life. People with anxiety disorders may experience physical symptoms such as sweating, trembling, and a rapid heartbeat, which can make it difficult to carry out daily tasks and activities. They may also avoid certain situations or activities because of their anxiety, which can lead to social isolation and further emotional distress.

Other mental health disorders, such as bipolar disorder, schizophrenia, and personality disorders, can also cause significant changes in mood and emotions. People with bipolar disorder may experience episodes of manic highs and depressive lows, while people with schizophrenia may experience delusions, hallucinations, and disorganized thinking. Personality disorders can cause difficulties in relationships, emotional instability, and impulsive behavior.

The emotional and behavioral changes associated with mental health disorders can be distressing and challenging to manage. They can interfere with an individual's ability to carry out daily tasks, maintain relationships, and engage in enjoyable activities. Seeking professional help, such as therapy and medication, can be an effective way to manage these changes and improve overall well-being.

- ***Distorting perceptions***

Schizophrenia is a chronic and severe mental health disorder that can cause a range of symptoms, including hallucinations, delusions, disorganized thinking, and abnormal behavior. Hallucinations and delusions are among the most prominent and distressing symptoms of schizophrenia, and can significantly impact an individual's perception of reality.

Hallucinations refer to sensory experiences that are not based on external stimuli. For example, people with schizophrenia may hear voices, see things, feel sensations, or smell odors that are not present. These hallucinations can be difficult to distinguish from reality and may cause significant distress, fear, and confusion. The voices or sounds that people with schizophrenia hear can be critical, demeaning, or commanding, and can interfere with their ability to think or concentrate.

Delusions, on the other hand, refer to false beliefs that are not based on reality. People with schizophrenia may believe that they are being persecuted, followed, or controlled by others, or that they have a special power or mission. They may also experience paranoid thoughts or ideas that people are trying to harm them. These delusions can cause significant anxiety, fear, and distress, and can make it difficult for individuals to carry out daily tasks or engage in social interactions.

Hallucinations and delusions can be particularly challenging to manage because they can be disruptive and distressing. They can also affect an individual's ability to communicate effectively, make decisions, and carry out daily tasks. Treatment for schizophrenia usually involves a combination of medication, psychotherapy, and support from family and friends to help manage symptoms and improve quality of life.

- ***Impairing cognitive functioning***

Mental health disorders can impact various aspects of cognitive functioning, which refers to the mental processes involved in attention, perception, memory, problem-solving, and decision-making. Cognitive deficits are common in many mental health disorders and can significantly affect an individual's daily life.

Attention-deficit/hyperactivity disorder (ADHD) is a neurodevelopmental disorder that can affect both children and adults. It is characterized by symptoms of inattention, hyperactivity, and impulsivity. People with ADHD may have difficulty sustaining attention, staying organized, completing tasks, and following through on instructions. They may also struggle with impulsivity, which can lead to risky behavior and poor decision-making.

Dementia is a progressive condition that affects memory, thinking, and behavior, and is most commonly associated with aging. People with dementia may experience significant memory loss and cognitive decline, which can interfere with daily activities such as managing finances, cooking, and communicating with others. They may also experience changes in mood and behavior and have difficulty with problem-solving and decision-making.

Other mental health disorders, such as depression, anxiety, and bipolar disorder, can also impact cognitive functioning. People with depression may have difficulty concentrating, making decisions, and remembering things. Anxiety can cause excessive worry and rumination, which can interfere with cognitive functioning and lead to poor decision-making. Bipolar disorder can cause changes in mood and energy levels that can affect attention, memory, and decision-making.

The impact of cognitive deficits on daily life can be significant, making it difficult to perform tasks, solve problems, and learn new information. Treatment for mental health disorders that impact cognitive functioning often involves a combination of medication and psychotherapy to manage symptoms and improve cognitive abilities. In some cases, cognitive rehabilitation and training may also help improve cognitive function.

- *Affecting behavior and motivation*

Mental health disorders can impact a person's behavior and motivation in several ways, depending on the specific disorder and individual. Changes in behavior and motivation can significantly impact a person's daily life, making it difficult to perform tasks, maintain relationships, and engage in enjoyable activities.

Depression is a mental health disorder that can cause a range of symptoms, including feelings of sadness, hopelessness, and worthlessness. It can also cause changes in behavior, such as a lack of motivation and energy. People with depression may have difficulty getting out of bed, completing daily tasks, and engaging in activities they used to enjoy. They may also withdraw from social interactions and have difficulty maintaining relationships.

Bipolar disorder is a mood disorder that is characterized by extreme changes in mood and energy levels. People with bipolar disorder may experience periods of mania, where they feel euphoric, have a decreased need for sleep, engage in risky behavior, and have inflated self-esteem. They may also experience periods of depression, where they feel sad, hopeless, and lack motivation and energy.

Other mental health disorders, such as anxiety and obsessive-compulsive disorder (OCD), can also impact behavior and motivation. People with anxiety may avoid certain situations or activities due to excessive worry and fear, which can interfere with daily life. OCD can cause compulsive behaviors and rituals that can be time-consuming and interfere with daily activities.

The impact of changes in behavior and motivation on daily life can be significant, affecting an individual's ability to carry out responsibilities, maintain relationships, and engage in enjoyable activities. Treatment for mental health disorders that impact behavior and motivation often involves a combination of medication and psychotherapy to manage symptoms and improve motivation and behavior. In some cases, behavioral therapies may also help address specific behaviors or habits that interfere with daily life.

- *Affecting physical health*

Mental health disorders can also have significant physical consequences that can impact a person's overall health and well-being. These physical symptoms can manifest in various ways, and the severity of the symptoms may vary depending on the type and severity of the mental health disorder.

Anxiety disorders, for example, can cause physical symptoms such as headaches, muscle tension, and gastrointestinal problems. People with anxiety disorders may experience symptoms such as rapid heartbeat, sweating, and shortness of breath, which can be distressing and interfere with daily activities. Chronic stress, which is often associated with anxiety disorders, can also have negative effects on physical health. It can increase the risk of cardiovascular disease, compromise the immune system, and contribute to other health problems such as obesity, diabetes, and gastrointestinal issues.

Depression can also have physical consequences. People with depression may experience changes in appetite and sleep patterns, which can lead to weight gain or weight loss and fatigue. Depression has also been associated with chronic pain conditions such as fibromyalgia, as well as an increased risk of cardiovascular disease.

Substance abuse disorders can also have physical consequences, such as liver damage, lung disease, and an increased risk of cancer. Substance abuse can also increase the risk of accidents and injuries, and contribute to long-term health problems such as hypertension, stroke, and mental health disorders.

The physical consequences of mental health disorders can have a significant impact on an individual's overall health and well-being. Treatment for mental health disorders that have physical consequences often involves a combination of medication and psychotherapy to manage symptoms and improve overall health. In some cases, lifestyle changes such as exercise, healthy eating, and stress reduction techniques may also be recommended to improve physical health and reduce the risk of long-term health problems.

It's important to note that mental health disorders can be treated, and seeking professional help is the first step toward recovery. Treatment may include medication, therapy, lifestyle changes, and support from friends and family.

7.2 *The role of Psychotherapy in Treating Mental health disorders*

Psychotherapy, also referred to as talk therapy, is a form of treatment that involves a therapeutic relationship between a trained mental health professional and an individual who is experiencing mental health problems. Psychotherapy is grounded in the principles of psychology, which is the study of human behavior, emotions, and cognition.

The goal of psychotherapy is to help individuals understand their thoughts, feelings, and behaviors to improve their mental health and well-being. Psychotherapy can be used alone or in combination with other treatments, such as medication, to manage a wide range of mental health disorders, including anxiety disorders, mood disorders, personality disorders, and others.

There are many different types of psychotherapy, each with its own set of principles, techniques, and goals. Some of the most common types of psychotherapy include:

- ***Cognitive-behavioral therapy (CBT)***

Cognitive-behavioral therapy (CBT) is a type of psychotherapy that focuses on changing negative patterns of thinking and behavior. CBT is based on the premise that our thoughts, feelings, and behaviors are interconnected, and that by changing our thoughts and behaviors, we can improve our mental health and well-being.

CBT is a short-term, goal-oriented therapy that typically involves weekly sessions with a mental health professional. During CBT, individuals learn to identify negative thought patterns, such as automatic negative thoughts or cognitive distortions, and replace them with more positive and realistic thoughts. Individuals also learn new coping skills and strategies for managing their emotions and behaviors.

CBT is an effective treatment for a wide range of mental health disorders, including depression, anxiety disorders, post-traumatic stress disorder (PTSD), obsessive-compulsive disorder (OCD), and others. Research has consistently shown that CBT is as effective as medication for many mental health disorders, and in some cases, maybe even more effective.

During a typical CBT session, individuals will work with their therapist to identify negative thought patterns and behaviors that are contributing to their mental health problems. They will then learn new coping skills and strategies for managing their thoughts and behaviors. Some common techniques used in CBT include:

1) *Cognitive restructuring:* This technique involves identifying and changing negative thought patterns, such as all-or-nothing thinking or catastrophizing.

2) *Behavioral activation:* This technique involves identifying and engaging in activities that promote positive emotions and behaviors.

3) *Exposure therapy:* This technique involves gradually exposing individuals to situations or stimuli that trigger their anxiety or fear, to help them learn to manage their symptoms.

4) *Relaxation techniques:* This technique involves teaching individuals relaxation techniques, such as deep breathing or progressive muscle relaxation, to help them manage their anxiety and stress.

CBT is often a collaborative process between the individual and their therapist, and individuals are often encouraged to practice the techniques they learn outside of therapy sessions. With practice, individuals can learn to identify and manage their negative thought patterns and behaviors, leading to improved mental health and well-being.

- ### *Psychodynamic therapy*

Psychodynamic therapy is a type of talk therapy that focuses on exploring the unconscious thoughts and emotions that may be influencing an individual's current thoughts, behaviors, and relationships. Psychodynamic therapy is based on the premise that our past experiences, particularly those from childhood, can shape our personality, emotions, and behaviors in adulthood.

During psychodynamic therapy, individuals work with a therapist to explore their unconscious thoughts and emotions, as well as their current relationships and behaviors. Through this process, individuals can gain insight into the underlying causes of their mental health problems and develop new ways of coping with their emotions and behaviors.

Psychodynamic therapy typically involves weekly sessions with a mental health professional and can last for several months or even years. During a session, individuals may be encouraged to explore their thoughts and emotions through free association, where they express whatever comes to mind without censorship or judgment. The therapist may also interpret the individual's dreams or other unconscious material to gain insight into their underlying thoughts and emotions.

One of the key goals of psychodynamic therapy is to help individuals develop a deeper understanding of their emotions and behaviors, and how these may be related to their past experiences. This can involve exploring early childhood experiences and relationships with parents or caregivers, as well as past traumas or conflicts that may be influencing their current thoughts and behaviors.

Psychodynamic therapy is often used to treat a variety of mental health conditions, including depression, anxiety disorders, personality disorders, and others. Research has shown that psychodynamic therapy can be an effective treatment for these conditions, particularly when it is tailored to the individual's specific needs and goals.

Overall, psychodynamic therapy can provide a safe and supportive space for individuals to explore their thoughts, emotions, and behaviors, gain insight into their underlying causes, and develop new coping strategies. It can be a long-term and intensive form of therapy, but can also be a highly effective treatment for a variety of mental health conditions.

- *Interpersonal therapy*

Interpersonal therapy (IPT) is a short-term, goal-oriented psychotherapy that focuses on improving an individual's interpersonal relationships and social functioning. IPT is based on the idea that our relationships and social interactions can significantly impact our mental health and well-being. The goal of IPT is to help individuals identify and address interpersonal problems and conflicts that may be contributing to their mental health problems.

IPT typically involves 12-16 weekly sessions with a mental health professional. During these sessions, the therapist and individual work collaboratively to identify and address interpersonal problems that are affecting the individual's mental health. The therapist helps the individual to develop specific goals for therapy and provides guidance and support in achieving those goals. IPT is based on four main areas of focus:

1) ***Grief and loss:*** This involves helping individuals process and cope with losses, such as the death of a loved one, a divorce, or other significant life changes. Grief and loss can significantly impact an individual's mental health, and IPT helps individuals to process their feelings and develop coping strategies.

2) ***Role transitions:*** This involves helping individuals adjust to significant life changes, such as starting a new job, getting married, or becoming a parent. These types of transitions can be stressful and can impact an individual's mental health. IPT helps individuals to identify and address the challenges associated with these transitions.

3) ***Interpersonal disputes:*** This involves addressing conflicts and disagreements with others, such as family members, friends, or co-workers. Interpersonal conflicts can be a significant source of stress and can impact an individual's mental health. IPT helps individuals to identify and address the underlying issues and develop strategies for managing these conflicts.

4) ***Interpersonal deficits:*** This involves helping individuals develop new skills and strategies for building and maintaining relationships, such as communication skills or assertiveness training. Interpersonal deficits can be a significant source of stress and can contribute to mental health problems such as depression and anxiety. IPT helps individuals to develop new skills and strategies for building positive relationships.

During IPT sessions, individuals may be encouraged to explore their feelings, thoughts, and behaviors related to these four areas of focus. The therapist may also provide guidance and support in developing new skills and strategies for managing interpersonal conflicts and building positive relationships. IPT is a collaborative and supportive form of therapy that focuses on helping individuals achieve specific goals related to their interpersonal relationships and social functioning.

Research has shown that IPT can be an effective treatment for a variety of mental health conditions, including depression, anxiety disorders, eating disorders, and others. IPT is often used in combination with medication and other forms of therapy, such as cognitive-behavioral therapy.

The effectiveness of IPT may be attributed to its focus on addressing interpersonal problems and conflicts, which can significantly impact an individual's mental health and well-being.

Overall, IPT can provide a supportive and collaborative environment for individuals to explore their interpersonal problems and conflicts, and develop new skills and strategies for managing their relationships and improving their mental health and well-being.

- ***Mindfulness-based therapy***

Mindfulness-based therapy (MBT) is a psychotherapeutic approach that integrates mindfulness practices and principles into the therapeutic process. The focus of MBT is to increase the individual's awareness and acceptance of present-moment experiences in a non-judgmental and compassionate way. It is based on the Buddhist tradition of mindfulness meditation, which has been adapted for use in Western psychotherapy.

The goal of MBT is to help individuals develop a greater awareness of their thoughts, feelings, and bodily sensations, and to learn to observe them without judgment. This can help individuals manage symptoms of anxiety, depression, stress, and other mental health conditions. MBT is effective in treating a range of mental health conditions, including anxiety disorders, depression, substance abuse, and chronic pain.

MBT typically involves weekly therapy sessions with a trained therapist who specializes in mindfulness-based therapy. During therapy sessions, individuals learn mindfulness practices and techniques, such as breathing exercises, body scan exercises, and meditation. They are also encouraged to practice these techniques regularly between sessions.

In addition to practicing mindfulness techniques, individuals may be encouraged to explore their thoughts and emotions related to their mental health condition. The therapist may also provide guidance and support in developing mindfulness practices and techniques to manage symptoms.

There are several different types of MBT, including Mindfulness-Based Stress Reduction (MBSR) and Mindfulness-Based Cognitive Therapy (MBCT). MBSR is a program that teaches individuals mindfulness practices to manage stress and improve well-being. MBCT is a program that combines mindfulness practices with cognitive therapy to help individuals manage depression and prevent relapse.

Research has shown that MBT can be an effective treatment for a variety of mental health conditions. For example, a meta-analysis of 39 studies found that MBT was associated with significant improvements in symptoms of anxiety and depression. Another study found that MBCT was as effective as medication in preventing relapse in individuals with recurrent depression.

Overall, psychotherapy works by providing a safe and supportive space for individuals to explore their thoughts and feelings. By talking with a mental health professional, individuals can gain insight into their patterns of thinking and behavior and learn new coping skills to manage their symptoms. Psychotherapy is also effective in helping individuals identify and change negative thought patterns, which can lead to improved mental health outcomes.

Research has shown that psychotherapy can be an effective treatment for many mental health disorders. For example, CBT is effective in treating depression, anxiety disorders, and PTSD. Psychodynamic therapy is effective in treating personality disorders and some forms of depression.

In some cases, psychotherapy may be used in combination with medication to manage symptoms. For example, individuals with severe depression or anxiety may benefit from both psychotherapy and medication.

Neuroscience and the Psyche

Overview

❖ **The Relationship between Neuroscience and the Psyche**

❖ **The Use of Neuroscience to Study the Psyche**

8.1 The Relationship between Neuroscience and the Psyche

As we have discussed earlier that the psyche, also known as the mind, is a complex and multifaceted concept that encompasses all aspects of human thought, emotion, behavior, and consciousness. It is the product of the activity of the brain and the nervous system, which work together to create the experiences that make up the psyche.

Neuroscience is the scientific study of the nervous system, including the brain, spinal cord, and nerves, as well as their functions and interactions with the body and the environment.

By studying the nervous system at various levels, from the molecular and cellular level to the systems and behavioral level, neuroscience provides insights into the biological mechanisms that underlie various aspects of the psyche.

One of the primary goals of neuroscience is to understand the neural basis of behavior and mental processes. This involves identifying the specific regions of the brain that are involved in various cognitive functions, such as perception, attention, memory, and decision-making.

For example, research has shown that the prefrontal cortex, a region of the brain located at the front of the forehead, is critical for executive functions, such as planning, working memory, and cognitive control.

Neuroscience also helps us understand the neural basis of emotions and how they are regulated by the brain. For example, studies have shown that the amygdala, a region of the brain involved in emotional processing, is particularly sensitive to negative emotional stimuli such as fear, and plays a role in regulating emotional responses.

Another important area of neuroscience research is the study of brain plasticity, or the brain's ability to change in response to experiences. This includes both short-term changes, such as the strengthening or weakening of connections between neurons, and long-term changes, such as the growth of new neurons and the formation of new neural pathways.

Brain plasticity is thought to be the basis of learning and memory, as well as the ability to adapt to new situations and environments.

Neuroscience research has also helped us understand the biological basis of mental health disorders. For example, studies have shown that individuals with depression have alterations in the functioning of certain brain regions, such as the prefrontal cortex and the hippocampus, as well as imbalances in certain neurotransmitters, such as serotonin and dopamine.

Similarly, individuals with anxiety disorders have been shown to have abnormalities in the amygdala and other regions involved in emotional processing.

However, it is important to note that the relationship between the brain and the psyche is complex and multifaceted, and cannot be reduced to a simple cause-and-effect relationship. While neuroscience research has provided valuable insights into the biological mechanisms underlying various aspects of the psyche, it is just one piece of the puzzle.

Other factors, such as environmental and social influences, personal experiences, and cultural context, also play important roles in shaping the psyche. Therefore, a comprehensive understanding of the relationship between neuroscience and the psyche requires an interdisciplinary approach that takes into account multiple levels of analysis, from the biological to the social and cultural.

8.2 *The Use of Neuroscience to Study the Psyche*

One of the main goals of using neuroscience to study the psyche is to identify the neural correlates of specific cognitive and behavioral processes. This involves using a variety of neuroimaging techniques to measure brain activity while participants engage in different tasks or experience different stimuli. One commonly used technique is functional magnetic resonance imaging (fMRI), which uses changes in blood flow to measure brain activity.

Another technique is positron emission tomography (PET), which measures changes in the uptake of radioactive tracers to identify areas of the brain that are active during a specific task or experience. Electroencephalography (EEG) is another method that measures the electrical activity of the brain using sensors placed on the scalp.

Using these techniques, researchers have identified many regions of the brain that are involved in specific cognitive and behavioral processes. For example, studies have shown that the prefrontal cortex, a region located at the front of the brain, is involved in decision-making, planning, and working memory. The amygdala, a small almond-shaped structure located deep in the brain, is involved in processing emotions such as fear and anxiety. The hippocampus, located in the temporal lobe, is involved in memory formation and retrieval.

Another important use of neuroscience in studying the psyche is to understand the neural basis of mental health disorders. Studies have used neuroimaging techniques to identify differences in brain structure and function between individuals with and without various mental health disorders, such as depression, anxiety, and schizophrenia. For example, studies have shown that individuals with depression have reduced activity in the prefrontal cortex, which may contribute to difficulties with decision-making and emotion regulation. Individuals with schizophrenia have been found to have abnormal brain activity in multiple regions, including the prefrontal cortex and the thalamus, which may contribute to their cognitive and perceptual symptoms.

Neuroscience has also been used to study the effects of experience on the brain and the psyche. Studies have shown that experiences such as learning, stress, and trauma can have profound effects on brain structure and function. For example, studies have shown that chronic stress can lead to structural changes in the hippocampus, which may contribute to difficulties with memory and emotion regulation. Studies have also shown that early life experiences, such as exposure to abuse or neglect, can have long-lasting effects on brain structure and function, as well as on the development of mental health disorders later in life.

Finally, neuroscience has been used to study the development of the brain and the psyche over the lifespan. Studies have shown that the brain undergoes significant changes during childhood and adolescence, as well as throughout adulthood and into old age. For example, studies have shown that the prefrontal cortex, which is involved in decision-making and impulse control, continues to develop well into the 20s and may not fully mature until the 30s or 40s. Studies have also shown that aging is associated with changes in brain structure and function, including reductions in gray matter volume and changes in the connectivity between different regions of the brain.

In conclusion, the use of neuroscience to study the psyche has provided valuable insights into the biological mechanisms underlying human cognition, emotion, and behavior. By identifying the neural correlates of specific processes and experiences, as well as the differences between healthy and disordered states, this field has the potential to inform the development of more effective treatments for mental health disorders and to promote healthy development across the lifespan.

However, it is important to note that neuroscience is just one piece of the puzzle and that a comprehensive understanding of the psyche requires an interdisciplinary approach that incorporates insights from psychology, sociology, anthropology, and other fields. Additionally, it is important to acknowledge the limitations of neuroimaging techniques and to interpret their results with caution. While these techniques can provide valuable information about brain activity, they do not provide a complete picture of the psyche, and it is important to consider the broader context in which psychological processes occur.

Furthermore, the use of neuroscience in studying the psyche also raises ethical concerns, particularly about the use of invasive techniques in animal research and the potential for the misuse of neuroscientific findings in areas such as criminal justice and marketing. Researchers and policymakers need to be mindful of these ethical considerations and to ensure that the use of neuroscience is guided by principles of transparency, accountability, and responsible use.

In summary, the use of neuroscience to study the psyche is a rapidly growing field that has provided valuable insights into the biological underpinnings of human cognition, emotion, and behavior. By identifying the neural correlates of specific processes and experiences, this field has the potential to inform the development of more effective treatments for mental health disorders and to promote healthy development across the lifespan. However, it is important to acknowledge the limitations of neuroimaging techniques, consider the broader context in which psychological processes occur, and be mindful of the ethical implications of this research.

Culture and the Psyche

Overview

* ❖ **The Impact of Culture on the Psyche**

  - ✓ *Identity formation*
  - ✓ *Worldview*
  - ✓ *Norms and Values*
  - ✓ *Emotional expression*
  - ✓ *Communication*

* ❖ **Cross-cultural Perspectives on the Psyche**

9.1 The Impact of Culture on the Psyche

Culture has a significant impact on the psyche, shaping our beliefs, values, behaviors, and perceptions of the world around us. The ways in which we understand ourselves, others, and the world are largely shaped by the culture in which we live. Here are some of how culture can influence the psyche:

- ***Identity formation***

Culture is a powerful force in shaping our sense of self and our understanding of our place in society. From a very young age, we learn from our families, communities, and broader cultural contexts about what it means to be a member of a particular gender, ethnicity, and social group.

These cultural messages inform our beliefs about ourselves, our values, and our behaviors, shaping our identity in multiple ways.

Gender identity is one example of how culture can shape our sense of self. Cultures have different expectations for how males and females should behave, dress, and interact with others.

These expectations can be subtle or overt, but they shape our understanding of what it means to be a man or a woman, and how we should act accordingly.

For instance, a culture that values traditional gender roles may expect men to be strong and assertive while women are expected to be nurturing and emotional. In contrast, a culture that values gender equality may encourage individuals to embrace a wider range of gender expressions and reject traditional gender stereotypes.

Ethnic identity is another way in which culture shapes our sense of self. Cultures have different expectations for how people of different ethnic backgrounds should behave, dress, and interact with others.

These expectations can include things like food, language, religion, and cultural practices. Our ethnic identity shapes our beliefs about ourselves, our attitudes toward others, and our behaviors in social situations.

Social identity is yet another way in which culture shapes our sense of self. Our social identity refers to the groups to which we belong and the roles that we play within those groups.

These groups can include family, friends, work colleagues, and others. Our social identity shapes our beliefs about ourselves, our values, and our behaviors within these groups, and it also influences our attitudes toward people outside of our group.

- *Worldview*

Culture plays a significant role in shaping our perception of reality and our interpretation of events and experiences. Our beliefs, attitudes, and values are heavily influenced by the cultural context in which we live. Here are some ways in which culture can shape our understanding of reality:

1. *Spirituality:* Culture plays a significant role in shaping our beliefs about spirituality and the supernatural. Different cultures have their own unique spiritual beliefs and practices, which can influence how individuals

perceive the world and its place in it. For instance, some cultures may believe in multiple gods or spirits, while others may believe in a single all-powerful deity.

2. *Morality:* Culture shapes our understanding of what is right and wrong. Different cultures have their unique moral codes and ethical principles, which can influence our attitudes toward certain behaviors. For example, some cultures may place a strong emphasis on individualism and personal freedom, while others may prioritize social responsibility and collective well-being.

3. *Meaning of life:* Culture can influence our understanding of the meaning of life and our purpose in the world. Different cultures may have different beliefs about what constitutes a fulfilling life and what goals individuals should strive for. For example, some cultures may prioritize the pursuit of wealth and success, while others may place greater emphasis on spirituality, community, and social connection.

4. *Interpretation of events:* Culture can also shape our interpretation of events and experiences. For example, different cultures may have different interpretations of mental illness, with some viewing it as a biological condition and others seeing it as a spiritual or moral issue. Similarly, different cultures may have different interpretations of history, with some emphasizing certain events or figures and others highlighting different aspects of the past.

Overall, culture plays a significant role in shaping our perception of reality and our interpretation of events and experiences. It is important to be aware of the cultural context in which we live to understand and appreciate the perspectives of others and to develop a more nuanced understanding of the world around us.

- *Norms and Value*

Culture plays a critical role in establishing the standards for acceptable behavior within a particular society. These standards guide our beliefs, values, and attitudes, and they shape our interactions with others. Here are some ways in which culture can set the standards for acceptable behavior:

1. *Social norms:* Culture defines the social norms that govern our behavior in various situations. These norms dictate how we should interact with others, what kind of language is appropriate, and what behaviors are considered acceptable in different contexts. For example, social norms may dictate that it is polite to say "please" and "thank you" or that it is inappropriate to talk loudly in public places.

2. *Moral values:* Culture shapes our understanding of what is right and wrong, and it establishes moral values that guide our behavior. These moral values may be based on religious beliefs or cultural traditions, and they can vary widely between different societies. For example, one culture may place a strong emphasis on honesty and integrity, while another culture may prioritize loyalty and obedience.

3. *Attitudes towards certain behaviors:* Culture also influences our attitudes towards certain behaviors. It can shape our understanding of what constitutes acceptable

behavior and what is considered taboo or inappropriate. For instance, some cultures may view alcohol consumption as a harmless social activity, while others may consider it a sign of moral decay.

4. ***Punishment for deviant behavior:*** Culture establishes the punishments for deviant behavior, which can include social ostracism, legal penalties, or even physical harm. These punishments serve as a deterrent to behavior that is considered unacceptable within a particular culture.

In summary, culture sets the standards for acceptable behavior within a particular society, and it establishes the moral and ethical principles that guide our interactions with others. By understanding these cultural norms and values, we can better appreciate the perspectives of others and navigate social situations more effectively.

- ***Emotional expression***

Culture plays a critical role in shaping how we express and perceive emotions. Here are some ways in which culture can influence our emotional expression and perception:

1. ***Emotional display rules:*** Culture can shape our emotional display rules, which are the cultural norms that govern how we express emotions in different social situations. These rules dictate what kind of emotional expressions are appropriate in different contexts, and they can vary widely between different cultures. For example, in some cultures, it may be considered appropriate to express anger or frustration openly, while in others, it may be considered inappropriate or even taboo.

2. ***Attitudes toward mental health:*** Culture can also shape our attitudes toward mental health and seeking help for emotional issues. Some cultures may view mental health issues as a sign of weakness or shame, while others may prioritize seeking help and support for these issues. These cultural attitudes can influence whether or not individuals seek help for emotional issues and the kind of support they are likely to receive.

3. ***Emotional experiences:*** Culture can also shape the way we experience emotions. For instance, some cultures may place a greater emphasis on expressing positive emotions such as joy and happiness, while others may prioritize emotional restraint and self-control. Similarly, some cultures may place a strong emphasis on the expression of negative emotions such as anger or sadness, while others may encourage emotional suppression and avoidance.

4. ***Emotional intelligence:*** Culture can influence our emotional intelligence, which is the ability to perceive, understand, and manage emotions effectively. Different cultures may prioritize different emotional skills, such as empathy, emotional self-awareness, and emotion regulation. These cultural differences can affect how individuals perceive and respond to emotions in themselves and others.

Overall, culture plays a critical role in shaping how we express and perceive emotions. By understanding these cultural differences, we can better appreciate the emotional experiences of others and navigate social situations more effectively. Additionally, understanding the cultural attitudes toward mental health can help us address and reduce the stigma surrounding emotional issues and improve access to mental health services.

• *Communication*

Culture plays a significant role in shaping how we communicate with others. Here are some ways in which culture can influence our communication:

1. *Language:* Culture shapes the language we use to communicate. Each culture has its own set of vocabulary, grammar rules, and pronunciation, which can make it challenging to communicate with people from different cultural backgrounds. For example, some cultures may place greater emphasis on formal language, while others may prioritize informal or colloquial language.

2. *Communication styles:* Culture can also influence our communication styles. Different cultures may prioritize different communication styles such as direct or indirect communication. Some cultures may prefer explicit communication, while others may prefer implicit or indirect communication. For example, in some cultures, it may be considered impolite to say "no" directly, while in others, it may be considered rude to avoid direct communication.

3. *Nonverbal cues:* Culture can also shape the way we use nonverbal cues such as facial expressions, gestures, and body language. Different cultures may attach different meanings to nonverbal cues, which can lead to miscommunication or misunderstandings. For example, in some cultures, maintaining direct eye contact may be considered a sign of respect and attentiveness, while in

others, it may be viewed as a sign of aggression or disrespect.

4. ***Communication norms:*** Culture can also establish communication norms that guide our interactions with others. These norms dictate how we should communicate in different situations and with different people, and they can vary widely between cultures. For example, some cultures may place a strong emphasis on interrupting others to show enthusiasm or agreement, while others may prioritize listening and allowing others to speak uninterrupted.

Overall, culture plays a crucial role in shaping how we communicate with others. By understanding these cultural differences, we can better appreciate the communication styles of others and adapt our communication accordingly. This can help us build stronger relationships with people from different cultural backgrounds and navigate diverse social and professional situations more effectively.

Overall, culture plays a significant role in shaping our psychological development and functioning. It can influence how we think, feel, and behave, and it is important to understand the cultural context in which people live to provide effective psychological treatment and support.

9.2 Cross-cultural Perspectives on the Psyche

Culture is a multifaceted construct that encompasses various aspects of the social, economic, political, and historical experiences of a group of people. Cross-cultural perspectives on the psyche suggest that culture can shape our understanding of mental health and illness. Cultural values, beliefs, customs, and practices influence our perceptions of psychological distress, the causes of mental illness, and the approaches to treatment and support.

One significant impact of cultural values on mental health is the way that different cultures view emotions and behavior. In some cultures, emotional expression is discouraged, and individuals may be expected to suppress their emotions. In contrast, in other cultures, emotional expression is valued, and individuals may be encouraged to express their emotions freely. These cultural expectations around emotional expression can significantly influence the way individuals understand and respond to psychological distress.

Culture also plays a significant role in the way that individuals seek help and support for mental health issues. In some cultures, seeking help for mental health issues is stigmatized or seen as a sign of weakness. This stigma can prevent individuals from seeking the help they need, leading to a lack of access to appropriate care. In other cultures, seeking help for mental health issues is seen as a sign of strength and resilience, and individuals may be more likely to seek support and treatment.

Spirituality and religion are also important cultural factors that can impact mental health. Many cultures view spirituality and religion as important components of psychological well-being, providing individuals with a sense of purpose, meaning, and connection to others. Practices such as prayer, meditation, and ritual can help manage stress and anxiety, improve mood, and enhance resilience.

Beliefs about the causes of mental illness can also differ across cultures. In some cultures, mental illness is viewed as the result of supernatural or spiritual causes, such as possession by demons or spirits. In other cultures, mental illness is seen as the result of biological or environmental factors. These cultural differences can influence the way that individuals understand and approach mental health issues, and can impact the effectiveness of treatment and support.

Cultural perspectives on mental health also influence the types of treatments that are considered acceptable or effective. In some cultures, traditional healing practices, such as herbal remedies or acupuncture, are viewed as effective treatments for mental health issues. Mental health professionals need to be aware of these cultural practices and be prepared to integrate them into their treatment plans if appropriate.

Finally, it is important to recognize that culture is not a static or fixed concept. Cultures can change and evolve, and individuals within a culture may have different beliefs and values. Mental health professionals need to be aware of these variations and adapt their practices to meet the needs of their clients. Developing culturally sensitive practices that take into account the diverse backgrounds and beliefs of their clients can lead to effective and appropriate care that supports the psychological well-being of all individuals, regardless of their cultural background.

The Future of the Study of the Psyche

Overview

❖ **Advances in the Study of the Psyche**

- ✓ *Cognitive psychology*
- ✓ *Neuroscience*
- ✓ *Positive psychology*
- ✓ *Developmental psychology*
- ✓ *Psychotherapy*
- ✓ *Cultural psychology*

❖ **The Future of the Study of the Psyche**

- ✓ *Artificial intelligence and machine learning*
- ✓ *Precision psychology*
- ✓ *Integrative approaches*
- ✓ *Virtual reality therapy*
- ✓ *The study of the microbiome*

10.1 Advances in the Study of the Psyche

There have been numerous advances in the study of the psyche over the years, as psychology has evolved and grown as a field. Here are some of the most notable advances:

- ***Cognitive psychology***

Cognitive psychology has made significant strides in understanding how people perceive, remember, and process information.

For example, researchers have discovered that attention can be selective, meaning that people are more likely to pay attention to things that are relevant to their goals and interests.

Cognitive psychology has also helped to develop new technologies, such as brain imaging techniques like functional magnetic resonance imaging (fMRI) that allow researchers to study the brain in action.

- ***Neuroscience***

Neuroscience has provided a more detailed understanding of the workings of the brain and how it relates to behavior, thoughts, and emotions.

Advances in neuroscience have led to the discovery of new neurotransmitters and receptors, as well as new methods for studying the brain, such as optogenetics, which uses light to control brain activity.

These discoveries have opened up new avenues for treating neurological and psychiatric disorders.

- ***Positive psychology***

Positive psychology is a relatively new field that aims to study positive aspects of human experiences, such as happiness, well-being, and optimal functioning.

This area of research has helped to shift the focus of psychology from solely studying problems and negative states to also promoting positive outcomes.

Positive psychology has led to the development of new interventions aimed at increasing well-being, such as gratitude journaling and positive affirmations.

- ***Developmental psychology***

Developmental psychology is concerned with understanding how people change and develop over time, from infancy to adulthood.

This field of research has helped to identify developmental milestones, such as when children first start to walk and talk, and how these milestones relate to cognitive and emotional development.

Developmental psychology has also helped to identify risk factors for developmental problems and disorders, such as autism and ADHD.

- ***Psychotherapy***

Psychotherapy is a broad field that encompasses a range of techniques aimed at improving mental health and well-being. Advances in psychotherapy have led to the development of new interventions, such as cognitive-behavioral therapy (CBT) and mindfulness-based interventions. CBT is effective in treating a range of mental health disorders, such as depression and anxiety, while mindfulness-based interventions have been shown to improve well-being and reduce stress.

- ***Cultural psychology***

Cultural psychology is concerned with how culture affects human behavior, cognition, and emotion. Advances in this field have helped to identify cultural differences in areas such as perception, emotion, and cognition.

For example, researchers have found that people from collectivistic cultures tend to prioritize the needs of the group over the needs of the individual, while people from individualistic cultures tend to prioritize individual needs and goals.

Cultural psychology has helped to promote cross-cultural understanding and has provided insights into how to work with people from diverse cultural backgrounds.

Overall, advances in the study of the psyche have allowed researchers to gain a better understanding of human behavior, emotions, and cognition. This knowledge can be applied to a variety of areas, such as mental health, education, and business.

10.2 The Future of the Study of the Psyche

The study of the psyche is a dynamic field that continues

to evolve and grow. Here are some potential areas of development for the future of the study of the psyche:

• *Artificial intelligence and machine learning*

AI and machine learning have the potential to help researchers analyze large datasets and identify patterns that may be difficult or impossible to detect with traditional statistical methods.

For example, researchers may use AI algorithms to identify biomarkers of mental health disorders, predict the course of a particular disorder, or develop personalized treatment plans for individuals.

Machine learning could also help identify patterns in brain imaging data that are associated with particular mental states or disorders.

• *Precision psychology*

Precision psychology takes into account an individual's unique genetic, environmental, and personal history to develop personalized interventions that are tailored to their specific needs.

For example, researchers may use genetic testing to identify individuals who are at higher risk for developing mental health problems and develop interventions that are designed to prevent the onset of those problems.

Precision psychology also aims to identify specific factors that may be contributing to an individual's mental health problems and develop interventions that target those factors.

- ### *Integrative approaches*

Integrative approaches aim to combine different fields of psychology to gain a more comprehensive understanding of the psyche.

For example, researchers may use brain imaging techniques to study the neural mechanisms underlying particular cognitive or emotional processes, such as decision-making or empathy. They may also use clinical psychology techniques to develop interventions that target those processes.

Integrative approaches may also help researchers understand the interactions between different systems in the body, such as the immune system and the brain.

- ### *Virtual reality therapy*

Virtual reality therapy involves using immersive virtual environments to help individuals confront their fears and anxieties in a controlled setting.

For example, individuals with post-traumatic stress disorder (PTSD) may be exposed to virtual environments that replicate the traumatic event to help them process and overcome their symptoms.

Virtual reality therapy has the potential to be more engaging and immersive than traditional forms of therapy, which may lead to better outcomes.

- ### *The study of the microbiome*

The microbiome refers to the community of microbes living

in and on the human body. Recent research has suggested that the microbiome may play a role in mental health, with some studies linking imbalances in the microbiome to disorders such as depression and anxiety. Researchers may use techniques such as fecal microbiota transplantation (FMT) to alter the microbiome to improve mental health outcomes. However, more research is needed to fully understand the role of the microbiome in mental health.

Overall, the future of the study of the psyche is exciting and holds great potential for improving our understanding of the brain and behavior, as well as developing new interventions for mental health problems. However, many challenges need to be addressed, such as ensuring that new technologies and approaches are accessible and affordable to everyone who needs them, and ensuring that research is conducted ethically and responsibly.

Summary

"Inside the Psyche" is a fascinating and in-depth exploration of the human psyche, covering its historical, structural, developmental, and cultural perspectives.

The book is an invaluable resource for anyone seeking to deepen their understanding of the complexities of human behavior, emotions, and mental health.

The book's introduction provides a concise and insightful definition of the psyche, emphasizing its importance in our daily lives.

From there, the book's historical overview of the study of the psyche takes readers on a journey through the evolution of psychology, tracing its roots from the early Greek philosophers to the modern-day pioneers of psychology, such as Freud and Jung.

Chapter three delves into the structure of the psyche, introducing readers to the different components of the psyche, including the conscious and unconscious mind, the ego, the id, and the superego. The chapter examines how these components interact with each other, providing readers with a deeper understanding of the psyche's inner workings.

Chapter four offers a fascinating look at the different stages of psychological development and how they shape the psyche. From infancy to adulthood, the book shows readers how various experiences and relationships influence the psyche and shape human behavior and emotions.

Chapter five examines psychological processes such as perception, attention, memory, emotions, motivation, and cognitive biases. The chapter explores how these processes contribute to shaping the psyche and offers insights into how they influence our daily lives.

Chapter six dives into different theories of personality and the relationship between personality and the psyche. The chapter examines how our personalities are shaped and how they relate to the different components of the psyche.

Chapter seven offers an in-depth examination of mental health disorders and their impact on the psyche. The chapter discusses the role of psychotherapy in treating these disorders and offers insights into how the psyche can be healed and restored.

Chapter eight provides an illuminating look at the relationship between neuroscience and the psyche, featuring how neuroscience is used to study the psyche, and its impact on our understanding of human behavior and emotions.

Chapter nine examines the impact of culture on the psyche, exploring cross-cultural perspectives and how culture shapes our understanding of the psyche.

Chapter ten explores advances in the study of the psyche, examining the future of psychology and the exciting new avenues of exploration it offers.

Finally, chapter eleven concludes the book, by summarizing key points and emphasizing the importance of understanding the psyche in our daily lives.

Overall, "Inside the Psyche" is an engaging and thought-provoking exploration of the human psyche, covering its various components, development, and cultural influences.

The book is an indispensable resource for anyone seeking to deepen their understanding of psychology and gain insights into the mysteries of human behavior and emotions.

Notes